Learning Disability and Contemporary Theatre

Great to see you here —
Kate & love
Rich

Jon

'This book is dedicated to all the actors who have worked with Full Body and the Voice and The Shysters over the last ten years, with thanks for their commitment and inspiration.'

Learning Disability and Contemporary Theatre:

Devised Theatre, Physical Theatre, Radical Theatre

Jon Palmer and Richard Hayhow

Published in 2008 by Full Body and the Voice
Lawrence Batley Theatre, Queen Square, Queen Street,
Huddersfield HD1 2SP
Full Body and the Voice is a Charity (1082267)and a Limited Company
registered in England and Wales (4015695).

http://www.fullbody.org.uk

Copyright © 2008 Jon Palmer and Richard Hayhow

The right of Jon Palmer and Richard Hayhow to be identified as the authors
of this work has been asserted by the author in accordance with the
Copyright, Designs and Patents Act 1988.

All rights reserved. Except for brief quotations in a review, this book, or
any part thereof, may not be reproduced, stored in or introduced into a
retrieval system, or transmitted, in any form or by any means, electronic,
mechanical, photocopying, recording or otherwise, without the prior
written permission of the publisher.

ISBN: 978-0-9561243-0-2

Typeset in Chaparral Pro by Sara Millington, Editorial and Design Services
Printed in Great Britain by CPI Antony Rowe, Chippenham, Wiltshire

Contents

List of Illustrations		*vi*
Foreword		*vii*
Introduction		1
I	Equality	11
II	Authenticity	33
III	Understanding the Person, Preparing the Actor	57
IV	Starting Points	85
V	Generating Material, Character and Narrative	107
VI	Visual Theatre: Structure, Narrative, Meaning	125
VII	Performance, Professionalism and the Public	151
Conclusion: Questions for the Future		173
Notes		183
Bibliography and Further Reading		189
Index		193

Illustrations

1. Actors from Belgium, France, Hungary and UK in the Culture 2000 project 'Zele du desir', directed by Jon Palmer.   x
2. Laura Sanchez and Lisa Carney in *Pinocchio*, York Theatre Royal.   10
3. Brian Haigh, Kevin Dyson and Peter Wandtke in *Knock Knock* by Full Body and the Voice.   32
4. Jon Tipton in *Pinocchio*, York Theatre Royal.   56
5. Development workshop with *Pinocchio* actors at York Theatre Royal.   77
6. Stage Exchange Workshop, York Theatre Royal.   77
7. Director Jon Palmer in rehearsals with actors from Full Body and the Voice.   84
8. Tasleem Hussain, Richard Ward, Kelvin Syme and Matthew Gosnay in *Scary Antics* by The Shysters.   106
9. Laura Sanchez, Robin Simpson, Peter Wandtke, Ben Langford and Vicki Hackett in *Pinocchio*, York Theatre Royal.   124
10. Jon Tipton in *Fallen Angels* by The Shysters.   150
11. Members of Full Body and the Voice Youth Theatre in a version of *The Tempest*.   172

Foreword

In the final years of the twentieth century two significant developments contributed to what director and author Clive Barker termed a 'silent revolution' in theatre: Jon Palmer was appointed Artistic Director of a new company, Full Body and The Voice, based in Huddersfield, and Richard Hayhow founded The Shysters, based in Coventry. Both directors worked with those companies for nearly ten years and both changed the British theatrical landscape. It is hard to overstate the impact of their work, occupying as they have a place in the vanguard of change in theatre involving people with learning disabilities.

This book, a collaboration between Jon and Richard, is not only a record of their experimentation and discovered methodologies but also a new insight into the central relationship between Director and Actor, the quest for 'authenticity', devising processes and an ongoing debate about the future for theatre in relation to performance by actors with learning disabilities.

Both directors had extensive experience before taking over the reins of the companies whose work is examined in this book. Jon Palmer, as Artistic Director of Interplay had developed techniques for unlocking creativity in young people with 'special needs' and Richard Hayhow's background in devised and community theatre had developed his ability to cohere groups in pursuit of a theatrical objective. Both men shared a fundamental belief that, with the provision of appropriate professional resources and an 'open' approach to theatre-making, actors with learning disabilities could create a new and radical theatre.

Since 1998 both men have steered their organisations through the choppy waters of social and theatrical change to challenge, engage and transform practice and attitudes surrounding the full engagement of people with learning disabilities as professional performers and theatre makers.

In order to contextualise the impact of the two directors' work it is necessary to consider the shape of British theatre before 1997, when Jon and Richard began their work with the two companies. With the exception, perhaps, of London-based GRAEAE, established in 1980 by Nabil Shaban and Richard Tomlinson, work made and performed by artists with disabilities tended to be local in terms of audience and ambition and to exist within the parameters of 'disabled theatre' with its inevitable minority arts label. Other theatre companies led by people with disabilities existed but did not generally produce work in larger or mainstream venues. They worked very much in a niche, usually involving project work or the occasional small-scale tour, playing most usually to audiences associated with the world of learning disability.

In mainstream theatre it was extremely rare if not unknown for actors with learning disabilities to appear alongside non-disabled performers, and whenever these actors did appear the work was frequently labelled 'special' – though more often it did not appear because the work was considered a commercial liability in terms of marketing. Audiences were then and are still largely today generally very underdeveloped in their knowledge and exposure to the creativity of actors with learning disabilities.

Both Jon and Richard have pushed the envelope in terms of the work they have developed and produced. From the outset The Shysters work has toured nationally (*Fallen Angels*, *Tango Apocolypso*, *Moses and the Two Tabs*), engaging audiences with its unique universality and non-text-based approachability. Full Body and The Voice similarly established itself as a touring and co-producing theatre company (*Knock Knock*, *Scene Changes*, *In the Footsteps of Mr Butler*).

With both companies moving in a similar trajectory, taking risks with both the audiences and their work, pushing acting by people with learning disabilities more and more into its rightful place in the mainstream, it seemed a natural step for Jon and Richard to collaborate in a co-production with Damien Cruden at York Theatre Royal. The resulting production *Pinocchio* (2007) was critically acclaimed and a benchmark in the evolution of truly integrated theatre.

This book not only asks searching questions about the future of theatre by actors with learning disabilities and the position of people with learning disabilities within society but it also provides a platform for both directors to describe exercises and artistic processes that will prove invaluable to practitioners and informative to every reader.

Many people have been involved in helping to bring this book to publication. These include some of the most talented theatre practitioners and academics currently involved in the creation of twenty-first-century theatre, who have generously contributed their observations and views on the role and history of theatre by actors with learning disabilities. Their insights have added value to the book's discourse. Contributors include Emma Rice (Artistic Director, Kneehigh), Phelim McDermott (Artistic Director, Improbable), Geraldine Ling (Artistic Director, The Lawnmowers) and Tom Shakespeare (NESTA Fellow, Newcastle University). Sincere thanks to them all for giving their views on creativity, the rehearsal and devising processes, theatre aesthetics, authenticity and performance.

I would also like to thank both Boards of Trustees for their support and determination to publish a book about the validity and importance of their companies' work that will sit within the historical canon of commentary charting the progress and direction of British theatre.

Special thanks to Susan Lawson who has studiously edited the text to produce this highly readable volume, to Maggie McEwan (Managing Director, Full Body and The Voice), who came up with the original idea for the book and sourced funding to make it happen, and to Lynda Hornsby, who liaised with all parties to help deliver a finalised publication. Last of all to The Arts Council England (Yorkshire) and Wesley Zepherin (Diversity Officer), who believed that a book like this needed to be written.

I commend this book to academics and students, practitioners, critics and anyone with an interest in cutting-edge contemporary theatre. I also want to thank every committed and dedicated professional across the country who has worked to bring the talents of actors with learning disabilities into the public domain for the rest of us to enjoy.

David Smith
Chair of Trustees, Full Body and The Voice

1. Actors from Belgium, France, Hungary and UK in the Culture 2000 project 'Zele du desir', directed by Jon Palmer. © 2003 Patrick Fabre.

Introduction

The last few years have seen a proliferation of literature on theatre practice outside of the mainstream. Devised theatre, visual theatre, even postmodern theatre and performance, once rarely documented beyond specialist journals, have found themselves the focus of analysis in dedicated student texts. Such theatres are now also widely studied within university departments, and their practices explored within drama schools. We might question the effects of such a shift on the subversive and experimental impulses at the core of much of this work, and some have noted the way in which students can tend to ape the most obvious elements of their visual styles, unwittingly substituting the perceived appearance of devised theatre for any true engagement with its processes. There is also the danger that academic criticism distances us from the live experience at the heart of the theatrical encounter. Nevertheless choosing to work from the margins should not and need not equate to 'marginalisation' and a counter-argument is that such analysis and documentation is essential if this work is to be fully understood, if it is to be taken seriously and if it is to reach wider audiences.

Disability and performance has also received attention of late. Whilst the practitioner or student wishing to read up in this area may not be inundated with volumes, they are also unlikely to leave a bookshop empty-handed. Disability Studies is now a recognised academic area and, since the beginnings of the disability movement, debate has shifted so far as to begin to question the movement's own earlier tenets. The presence of actors with physical impairments in the world of theatre is now, one hopes, fully acknowledged, as is the way in which physical impairment challenges outdated ideas about the body in performance. Work informed by identity politics has challenged the neutrality of the body and contemporary performance is engaged with the notion of the embodied performer; the actor's body is no longer perceived as neutral territory through which pass the playwright's characters like a series of phantoms.

Yet the reader or practitioner seeking to find a book about theatre made by actors with learning disabilities will be frustrated. Whilst there is an admirable and growing body of literature on learning disability, and also on drama therapy and other therapeutic applications of drama, professional theatre made by actors with learning disabilities seems barely acknowledged, indeed invisible, if the content of bookshops is taken to reflect public awareness. As we write this Introduction, a number of professional screen actors with learning disabilities are attracting attention in the broadsheets, whilst a hard-hitting London billboard campaign recently addressed the fact that employers currently do little to welcome employees with Down Syndrome – with a mere 16 per cent of those with Down Syndrome given the opportunity to work. It is shocking that this should be the case in 2007; furthermore those few actors with learning disabilities who have found professional television work are inevitably cast in programmes addressing learning disability per se. Yet actors with learning disabilities can and do make professional work – and on a broad range of themes. This book is testament to the fact.

Our remit is to ask *why* such work has gone unacknowledged, to document the fact that it exists and to explore its unique qualities; most importantly, however, we are interested in discussing how such work has been made and performed and how it might be more widely facilitated in the future. Drama schools have been slow to catch up in this respect and there is still no formal training available for actors with learning disabilities to match that available to the actor without learning disabilities. This book, then, also provides for directors what the drama schools have thus far failed to provide for actors. The director seeking to work with actors with learning disabilities in a professional context will need to take on, to an unprecedented extent, the role of trainer as well, within the development of any production or project. The methods, however, will be radically different. We would go so far as to say that what is learned from working with actors with learning disabilities about the art of theatre might be fruitfully applied to drama training on a more general level.

Actors with learning disabilities who have featured in dramas *about* learning disability have received (limited) attention, as we have noted. Beyond the few professional screen actors who have managed to find employment, there are also those theatre companies whose work has been immensely valuable in raising issues around the visibility of those with learning disabilities and the ways in which mainstream theatre tends to exclude audience members with learning disabilities, both in content and in terms of pragmatics. We must also, however, promote the right of the actor with a learning disability to make work on any given theme. Is it inconceivable that he or she might have something to say beyond this one particular aspect of his or her life? Or indeed that he or she might wish to engage with wider social issues, or even to eschew political theatre in the first place? In short is it inconceivable that those with a learning disability might wish, quite simply, to be actors?

The notion of 'learning disability theatre', a catch-all term used to describe any work made by actors with learning disabilities, has in the past been useful in terms of raising awareness. We would argue that the term is perhaps now redundant, if not in fact problematic. Furthermore it is of little use to the aspiring professional actor with learning disabilities who wishes not to be constrained by this very 'disability'. The authors' companies are just two whose members all have learning disabilities, ranging from autism to Down Syndrome, and who have come together in order, quite simply, to make professional theatre. In our experience the 'learning disability theatre' label does little to encourage audiences to seriously engage with these actors' work. On the contrary, it may even undermine it.

For us, learning disability appears to be the final frontier of both theatre and identity politics. Devised and experimental theatre has tackled numerous prejudices and has been, on the whole, and at least in its early days, highly politically vocal. Yet in contrast to physical disability (despite ongoing social issues of access, prejudice, lack of facilities and the pernicious wider ideology of 'tragedy'), learning disability, it seems, remains taboo. This situation prevails, we would argue, in part due to a deeply problematic stigma around 'mental illness', with which learning disability is frequently confused. Perhaps more crucially, the skills that are affected in learning disabilities – the ability to 'conceptualise', language acquisition, sequencing, verbal eloquence – remain highly prized within our society and, particularly, within the world of theatre. Yet there is a conundrum here. If radical devised theatre sought to escape the impositions of scripted models and 'logical' or realist linear narratives, if it also sought to get back to the true theatrical impulse, which is above all sensory, emotional, authentic, and bodily, the seeming invisibility of work by actors with learning disabilities becomes instead a sort of blind spot. It is interesting in this respect how often devised theatre, in seeking to escape these realist and rational models, is ultimately constructed through processes that rely on the very things its narratives aim to avoid.

This book seeks to redress the absence of documentation and discussion of professional theatre practice by actors with learning disabilities. In line with the nature of the work under consideration, we do not aim for a conceptualised or academic thesis and have written this book with students and, perhaps primarily, practitioners in mind. If the processes we describe also sound therapeutic at times, this is because the development of the actor is, for us, essential to the development of profound theatrical work. Yet this is not the primary aim, and we do not shirk from arguing for the necessity of such work to be considered in the light of what it is – professional practice. This is not then a book about what theatre can bring to those with learning disabilities; rather it is a book about what actors with learning disabilities can bring to theatre.

We emphasise above all the organic nature of the devising process. The layout of the book reflects as much as is possible this organic process, beginning with a context for the work and outlining the basic premise for good theatre – for us, authenticity. We then move into the studio – the setting for the central portion of this book – and finally back to the wider world, through discussion of professional performance in the face of critical and discerning audiences. Nevertheless a book must have a linear narrative that is perhaps more rigid than the natural flow of studio work. For clarity, a book must also be divided into chapters. We have therefore tried to mirror the flow of theatre-making processes whilst bearing in mind the need to break down these processes into loosely chronological and digestible stages.

We begin in Chapter I by looking in-depth at the notion of equality, whose seemingly obvious meaning belies the existence of opposing understandings of the term, and the ways in which this has been understood by theatre-makers during the last third of the twentieth century and into the twenty-first. Devised theatre abandoned traditional hierarchies along with text-based models and the work discussed stems from this movement. Acknowledging the importance of community theatre and therapeutic drama, as well as the work of professional theatre groups who tackle learning disability advocacy, this chapter proposes a further level of 'equal access' to theatre: access to theatrical vision itself. Outlining the birth of devised and experimental theatre and its relationships to the equal rights movements and identity politics, we suggest not only that people with learning disabilities can be professional actors but that, as professionals, they bring to theatre unique theatrical forms.

In Chapter II we focus on the centrality of authenticity to meaningful performance, placing our discussion within the wider context of the quest for 'authenticity' in twentieth century and contemporary theatre practice. If authenticity requires us to reach beyond mediated or 'false' behaviour and imposed social codes, we ask how authentic it is possible to be as a socialised being and to what extent linguistic skills and societal structures camouflage our authentic selves. Learning disability is generally understood in the negative, as an inability to acquire certain skills of language and socialisation; we instead focus on the ways in which this 'inability' facilitates more direct theatrical expression. The chapter also addresses the notion of embodied performance and the way in which performer and character collide in experimental theatre to cut through inauthentic representation of imposed roles.

Having established the context for and the underpinning of the work we then move into the studio. Chapter III discusses the importance of preparation and of getting to know the actors, of building rapport and trust within an ensemble company. Due to the current lack of formal training for actors with learning disabilities, a director working with those with learning disabilities will need to begin at the beginning. We therefore look at the earliest aspects of making theatre, including ways of removing blocks to authenticity and freeing up the actor; confidence-building; physical and vocal exploration, and warm-up techniques. Emphasising the importance of non-verbal communication, as well as the shared shaping of the theatrical vision, we also discuss the importance of the director's receptivity, empathy and integrity in relation to the actors' early creative work.

In the work discussed in Chapter IV we begin to make theatre proper. Considering a number of starting points, we discuss the use of objects, music, images and even places in the early stages of theatre-making. We emphasise particularly the power of objects and of music, both live and pre-recorded, to stimulate theatrical expression and to provide an external focus for internal states. In Chapter V we cover various techniques for generating theatrical material. For us theatrical motifs, stories and characters are not superimposed upon the actors but instead emerge organically in an unearthing process that we liken to excavation. From the hands-on role of the director emphasised in the previous chapters, working beside and with the actors, we discuss the director's shift from full collaborator to 'translator' of the emerging work. Techniques for generating material include repetition and layering, character and relationship exploration and the complete collaboration of the actors in the work.

Unlike the linear storylines of conventional theatre, the narratives that emerge in work with actors with learning disabilities tend, in our experience, to be visual, sensory and impressionistic, echoing the experiments of 'visual theatre' and physical theatre that have flourished since the 1960s. Chapter VI is concerned with the way in which such material is framed or shaped into a final vision, with the director stepping still further back to become an 'editor' or mediator and, indeed, the first member of the audience. Here we distinguish between plot and narrative and consider the notion of 'poetic juxtaposition'. We look at precedents for such non-linear narratives and at the ways in which visual and poetic theatre produces meaning. Finally we emphasise the importance of achieving 'readability' for an audience whilst avoiding insensitive imposition and ensuring that the actors retain ownership of the final work.

Having produced a piece of theatre, the ensemble must at last take to the stage. The final chapter emerges from the studio to address the wider performance context and the relationship with audiences. By contrast with therapeutic models, we note the importance of ambition and discernment for professional actors with learning disabilities. In conclusion we grapple with the way such work is marketed and toured and suggest that theatre-goers and critics may need to redefine their own parameters in order to approach and understand this radically experimental work and in order to move beyond restrictive notions of 'learning disability theatre'. Looking to the future, we ask what drama schools will need to do in order to redress the crucial issue of access, especially in the face of wider visibility and employment opportunities for actors with learning disabilities.

We hope that this book serves as a useful and readable guide for any theatre practitioner wishing to enable dynamic work with professional actors with learning disabilities. The methods are unconventional, since they have been developed organically and in the studio through hands-on work. Actors are at the very heart of theatre and our model of practice steers clear of imposition at all costs; the methods we propose therefore stem directly from the actors' skills and working preferences. We do not however suggest that our model is definitive, nor are we advocating a rigid methodology – there may well be other ways of working that have yet to be developed. In developing our approach we have acted like magpies, taking exercises and games from many sources, being open to influence by all sorts of practitioners and adapting and inventing on the spot as feels appropriate. There are many excellent books on the market that elaborate on particular methodologies – we suggest useful sources at the end of this book. We have also kept our descriptions of games to a minimum, in part because other books serve this purpose and in part to encourage the reader to work out their own ways of doing things.

Finally, in writing this book we hope to encourage and facilitate the work of many more actors with learning disabilities in the future.

As more practitioners with learning disabilities come together to make professional theatre, the approaches taken and the work produced will undoubtedly shift and grow, taking directions we cannot yet imagine. This book, we hope, is only the beginning.

2. *Laura Sanchez and Lisa Carney in* Pinocchio, *York Theatre Royal.*
© *2007 Karl Andre.*

1
Equality

With the radical overhaul of theatre practices in the last third of the twentieth century and in a variety of other ways drama has been wrested from the theatres of the mainstream and made available to all members of society – including those with learning disabilities. Community theatre and, particularly, therapeutic drama has brought theatre to those with no previous theatrical knowledge or training, providing the chance for personal expression within a form once strictly reserved for the 'chattering classes'. For those with learning disabilities – either mild or profound – drama, like other creative forms, has been usefully divorced from notions of training, quality and ambition. Such work has been and remains invaluable for a variety of reasons. Yet we must also ask the question: where does this leave the person with learning disabilities who wishes to become a professional actor?

Notions of professionalism and discernment have been understood rather differently by facilitators of applied theatre from practitioners of mainstream theatre and, since it is usually assumed that those with learning disabilities do not entertain thoughts of professional participation in the arts, the question is rarely raised. Assumptions about the nature of learning disabilities – that those with autism do not have imagination, for example – as well as about the nature of professional theatre as primarily understanding and delivering text, acquiring skills and representing characters have also tended, in many people's minds, to bar the possibility of actors with learning disabilities from participating professionally. For us, given the drive towards the democratisation of culture and the focus on equality that shook the theatre world in the 1960s and 1970s, this remains a curious situation.

This shake-up of theatre practice stemmed in large part from the political climate of that era. These decades saw a flowering of new and experimental forms and a proliferation of theatre groups who began to make (or 'devise') theatre together, often without a director and certainly without a script pre-written by an absent playwright. Of the large number of companies and collectives who began devising theatre, including those from performance art backgrounds, many focused on creating new 'visual languages' of theatre. Others were more clearly political in nature, and the devising format allowed for mutual experimental development of works on political themes. In all cases the hierarchical relationships and rigid roles of conventional theatre were broken down. Many groups also aimed, at least in principle, to break down the rigid distinctions between actors and spectators, and to make work for wider and more varied audiences whose diversity had now begun to be recognised.

Whilst some of the early groups had a clear socialist agenda, the 1970s and 1980s saw the emergence of theatre groups inspired by the Civil Rights and Women's Liberation movements and a new shift towards identity politics. Equal rights in theatre meant theatre made by those groups was traditionally marginalised by the mainstream. These newly formed ensembles also often chose to use theatre as a forum in which to make work with identity politics as its theme. Within this climate, in which women's theatre groups, gay and lesbian theatre groups and black and Asian groups flourished, companies such as Graeae, whose actors all have physical disabilities, also began to make work about their situation in a political vein. Inspired by the advances in equal rights legislation, the disability movement began to question assumptions that saw the individual as disabled by his or her physical impairment, instead arguing that 'the problem of disability is externally located and that our exclusion from society is a human rights issue.'[1] While this position – known as the 'social model' of disability – has recently been questioned for its limits in acknowledging those difficulties in life (for example, medical problems) actually caused by physical impairments, it was nevertheless crucial in pushing for better access and facilities for people with physical impairments.[2] The social model also highlighted the numerous ways in which society undermined or made impossible access to mainstream community involvement for those with learning disabilities, including involvement in art forms such as theatre.

Learning disability was barely on the radar until the 1980s, however, with the emergence of the notion of 'special needs' and of special schools set up to cater for those needs, so general awareness of learning disability was still limited during the very era in which equal rights issues and identity politics were at their most prominent. Furthermore because of the nature of learning disability, primarily perceived as an absence of certain crucial skills, and because these 'disabilities' by definition affect verbal eloquence, even those aware of learning disability generally failed to locate it within an equal rights framework. The possibility of those with learning disabilities wishing to make work as professional artists, therefore, was also barely thinkable. Nevertheless, theatre companies were being formed that provided opportunities for people with learning disabilities to explore drama as a means of personal expression. The reasons for the emergence of these groups were many and varied, ranging from a politically driven concept of equality of access to mere happenstance. Much of this work was, and is, concerned to a large extent with advocacy and has been invaluable in raising awareness of learning disability and in allowing wider participation in drama.

Increased awareness of learning disability also coincided with the development of the community theatre and theatre-in-education (TIE) movements. With the more overt political agendas of the early socialist ensembles increasingly redirected into the community arena, obvious political statements were abandoned in favour of the democratisation of access. Community theatre therefore generally drew on issues of local interest for its themes, as well as tailoring its content to the styles thought most likely to interest the intended viewers. For those with learning disabilities this access came primarily through TIE programmes, with theatre being toured to special schools. The most interesting of this work is able to engage the audience on its own terms.[3] Too much of it, however, especially in the case of audiences with profound and multiple learning disabilities, tends to assume little more than the need on the part of the students for a cosseting environment. The development of 'sensory rooms', safely padded and with coloured lights and soft music, also aimed for the provision of a 'fantasy environment' in which one could be rocked or rolled without the slightest physical risk and in direct contrast to the rude realities of the world outside the school. Engagement of the senses, on its own, does not necessarily equate to drama, and we would argue from experience that it is possible to go beyond this model to imbue the work with what we might call a form of 'sensory narrative'. Such work stimulates the senses in the service of a wider context of 'storytelling', understood in its broadest, non-literary sense.

Those with milder forms of learning disability thus began in the 1980s to be enabled to work with drama as a forum for 'playing out' personal issues, within drama therapy for example, or alternatively to make professional work whose themes and contents primarily addressed issues around learning disability itself. Those on the more severe end of the learning disability spectrum, where they have had access to theatre at all, have too often been provided with a type of theatre which is in fact little more than stimulus and which can tend to have very little dramatic potential; the best of this work transcends this limitation. What has been crucial in both cases, however, is the notion of equality of access to theatre.

We would like to introduce another notion of equality, however: equality of access to *theatrical vision* and, alongside that, to professional practice as an actor. For us the two are intertwined: by access to vision we mean the opportunity to create the kind of theatre that best suits the actor's own skills and inclinations, a position which is usually taken for granted by those making devised theatre. Our own work has been concerned to broaden the actors' (and by implication audiences') awareness of the range of theatre aesthetics; we have wanted to train creative actors who are skilled in improvising and devising, rather than endeavouring to shoehorn the actors into learning how to 'perform' within conventional theatre models. Equality of access to theatrical vision is also about opening up and extending what we take to be the 'normal' means of communication. We are interested in validating unconventional (or, more accurately, non-normative) ways of seeing and being in the world, especially since the worldviews of people with learning disabilities have been perceived as flawed or abnormal, where they have been perceived at all. Since this approach to theatrical vision stems directly from, and is indeed part of, the devised theatre movement rather than conventional theatre practice, it will be useful to outline in more depth the radical developments in theatre practices since the 1960s and 1970s. The history of devised theatre, as we noted in the Introduction, is increasingly of wider interest. As such much of it has been documented in recent years. Due to its centrality in enabling the emergence of the unique theatrical forms currently being created by professional actors with learning disabilities, it is nevertheless worth summarising the development of the form.

Why Make Devised Theatre? Politics and Vision

For a generation of actors trained to delve deeply into the psychology of their characters, rather than to re-present the external effects of a particular emotion, and with the improvisation techniques of Keith Johnstone and others increasingly in circulation in drama training in the late 1970s, the hierarchical substructure of mainstream theatre had already begun to crumble. In the studio, actors and other theatre-makers now demanded greater input and involvement in the whole theatre-making process, no longer content to take instructions from a distant director behind a desk about characters imposed on them through age-old scripts. Control of the work was wrested from the hands of individual directors and playwrights. In the wider world, too, profound changes were underway. This was a highly politicised generation for whom bourgeois art forms exemplified all that was rotten within societal structures. Compelled to break down the barriers between play and actor, actor and audience, and to restore to theatre the basic essence of the dramatic encounter, it was inevitable that theatre must undergo profound changes. With stage censorship also having been abolished in 1968, ever more political issues had begun, quite literally, to take centre stage.

The earliest political companies working in the UK were overt in their agenda: these were socialist theatre companies for a socialist climate, with union action at its peak and 'class warfare' a widespread battle cry. For companies working in an overtly political vein – most particularly the Agitprop Street Players (later Red Ladder), formed in 1968 – theatrical aesthetics were, at least initially, low on the list of priorities. The Agitprop Street Players made short works for specific scenarios that involved simple slogans and easy-to-grasp political metaphors. Devised agitprop pieces were inexpensive to make and, as Deirdre Heddon and Jane Milling note, 'They were also capable of being adapted quickly in response to real events. This is one advantage of the devised script; having been devised and performed by the group, it could quickly be revised and kept up to date.'[4] Other UK groups with a clear political emphasis included Unity Theatre, CAST (Cartoon Archetypical Slogan Theatre), North West Spanner, 7:84 and their offshoot Belt and Braces, Mutable Theatre, The Bradford Art College Theatre Group and Welfare State International, whose work developed as an interesting hybrid of celebratory community theatre and a very particular brand of socialist ideology. By the 1970s, single-pronged socialist politics had largely been displaced by identity politics. Feminist groups such as Monstrous Regiment and Women's Theatre Group (re-branded in 1991 as Sphinx) and lesbian and gay groups such as Siren and Gay Sweatshop tended to have a particular slogan, issue or ethos. Identity politics was not limited to gender and race, however. The theatre group Age Exchange (amongst others) worked and continues to work to challenge the invisibility of the elderly in our communities, whilst learning disability groups, late on the scene, continue to use theatre as a political forum.

Overt politics are not the only impetus for devising theatre, however, and if our own stance may be said to be political it is in the wider sense of advocating the right to creative expression. In this respect the work of those early collectives whose aim was primarily the communal exploration of theatrical form are of equal importance. These included, amongst others, the People Show (perhaps the most well-known and certainly the longest-running devised theatre group in the UK) who began collaborating in 1966. Others included IOU (a group of performers who split from Welfare State International in 1976) , Hesitate and Demonstrate, Blood Group and the Theatre of Mistakes, whose work, influenced both by minimalism and the 'post-minimalist' performance of artists such as Robert Wilson, took repetitive functional actions (and their inevitable failures) into the London streets. Often referred to as 'visual theatre', 'image theatre' or even 'performance art theatre' due to its crossover with the Happenings and performance art simultaneously flourishing in the visual art arena, this work utilised the group format to forge wholly new visual and bodily 'languages'. The work of these groups often combined music, visuals and improvisation and tended to emphasise physicality and visual impact over verbal or script-led forms.

Many of the founders and members of these groups had visual arts backgrounds, whilst the visual arts at this time were also drawing on early theatrical traditions. As well as exploring new visual languages, both actors and artists working in this way were interested in the uniquely 'live' quality of theatre and in the potential authenticity of performance when stripped of its traditional theatrical conventions – an authenticity that is also key to the work under discussion in this book, which will be explored in-depth in the following chapter. As against the mainstream re-presentation of character-led roles, these performers were interested instead in presenting work in which the line between actor and character was blurred – and indeed in some cases it disappeared altogether. They were interested too in dissolving the boundaries between the actors/artists and the audience. Whilst the level to which the spectator meaningfully participated in Happenings and other performance events varied greatly, performance art and other crossover forms nevertheless succeeded in opening up the experience to *potential participation* and to the vagaries of chance. In doing so it drastically decreased the performer's ability to rely on a pre-planned or scripted scenarios and shifted the emphasis further from 'acting' as pretence to 'acting' as 'doing'.

The search for new forms of 'visual narrative' may seem to lack the social engagement of the political ensembles, despite rejecting conventional mainstream or bourgeois theatre. In the fact that it also places emphasis on the final theatrical product and its attendant aesthetic, in contrast to the emphasis on process and participation in community and therapeutic theatre, it may even seem conventional. Yet the exploration of new 'languages' of theatre is, for us, inherently political, since in order to express radically new worldviews it is surely necessary to seek out new languages in which to present them. These visual languages have for the most part been perceived as bodily, and in many ways understood as rebelling against the 'tyranny of words' – the way in which we have come to see verbal and written language as the primary and most effective means of communication.[5] Without doubt this is what the influential theatre director Peter Brook set out to do when, in 1972, under the auspices of the Centre for International Theatre Research, he embarked on the 'Conference of the Birds' project. Gathering together an international group of actors, Brook set out across Africa in an attempt to rediscover the essence of the theatrical encounter. The group would arrive in a remote African village, unroll a carpet in the main square to define a performance space and begin an improvisation in the hopes of attracting an audience. The purpose was to see that to which the audiences did or did not respond; to discover whether there was such a thing as a universal theatre language. By definition this 'language' could not be verbal, since verbal language would necessarily be a barrier to communication in an international venture of this sort.

Brook is not the only director to have been acutely aware of the ways in which the theatrical form itself affects its meaning and its ability to 'speak' in other (non-conventional) 'voices'. Others, such as Anna Furse, have also explored the way in which new meanings or voices may require more than just a forum. Using her company Blood Group not to speak conventionally about the issues in which they were interested (in this case, women's subjectivity) but to discover new 'feminine' theatrical languages, Furse proposed instead a 'language of the body'.[6] Within our own experience of working with those with profound and multiple learning disabilities, we would have had little choice *not* to reconsider traditional narrative formats. Yet even working with professional actors with less severe forms of learning disability, the 'language' of theatre that emerges is clearly different to that of traditional mainstream theatre. For us the ability to 'speak' or act in one's own expressive language *is* a political issue.

Ironically, by the mid-1980s, those companies who had once rejected the importance of aesthetic criteria in favour of relaying a political message had also begun to realise that, regardless of the importance of the message, it would only reach people if the medium in which it was presented was also of theatrical interest. Even the most dedicated of political and 'agitational' companies began to reconsider their stance and to concentrate anew on making visually exciting theatre. For this reason the shift in their methods has been perceived as part of a re-professionalisation of radical theatre:

> This focus on the production, over process, implies an equal or greater degree of concern with the cultural value of the work than with its political impact, or at the least, it suggests a different way of relating 'politics' to 'product' by suggesting that practitioners were becoming more critical of the forms through which politics were being presented.[7]

A return to formal concerns did not always produce radical results, however; by the 1980s much political theatre had become increasingly traditional in format. For Heddon and Milling:

> plays written for those collaborative companies that still survived certainly approached the conditions of more conventional – or bourgeois – theatre ... By the 1980s any explicit political signifiers that remained were to be found not in radical modes of production but instead in the content of plays, although by now these politics were far removed from the socialist politics of work produced in the 1970s.[8]

Nevertheless interesting 'visual' and physical theatre continued – and continues – to be made. In fact, and perhaps ironically, primarily visual or mixed-media theatre, and the work of physical theatre groups such as Complicite, inspired by the French director Jacques Le Coq, have even become the 'mainstream' form for independent audiences.

Certainly the use of popular rather than highbrow theatrical tropes such as mime, *commedia dell'arte* and vaudeville are political to the extent that they re-popularise – give back to the people – the theatrical tradition. For overtly political theatre the impetus has dissolved under the pressure of economic and funding restraints, amongst other factors. Its drive towards democratisation can still be found, however, in community theatre, to which many companies turned in the shifting political and economic climates of the late 1970s and 1980s.

Community Theatre, Drama as Therapy and the TIE Movement

By 1975 the UK had what Chris Johnston describes as a 'fledgling community theatre movement',[9] with drama's focus now shifted from the needs of the audience to those of the actors or participants. This included the work of Word and Action (Dorset), Inter-Action, and Banner Theatre amongst others. Influenced by Keith Johnstone's improvisation methods (as well as Augusto Boal's *Theatre of the Oppressed*, newly arrived in the UK) these companies had 'real commitment to building relationships with working-class and disenfranchised communities',[10] and performed not in theatres but in venues as diverse as factory canteens, prisons and community centres. Many such companies, including CAST, Belt and Braces, and Recreation Ground had started out with clear socialist or class-politics focused agendas. The move towards community theatre in a sense returned them to their roots, making theatre for those least likely to engage in traditional 'bourgeois' theatre-going. Contrary to the anti-establishment ethos of the majority of the devised theatre companies, however, the growth of the community theatre movement was to a large extent influenced by the provision of government funding. For the first time since the radical overhaul of theatre in the 1960s, both the establishment, and those who had questioned it, seemed to be working towards the same aim: the encouragement and facilitation of wider participation in theatre.

Community work's motivation, at least on the part of the makers, was to give the power (of art) back to the people or, on a more pragmatic level, to improve their local communities either socially or in real terms. The stated aim of Inter-Action Theatre, founded in 1968, for example, was 'to involve people in the improvement of their own communities, making them better places to raise their children and join with other adults to provide leisure and recreational facilities'.[11] Here the content of the drama – as well as traditional notions of performance – are almost beside the point. Many practitioners in community theatre – and, more generally, community arts – held and still hold dear to the notion of some sort of political content or purpose, primarily through allowing participants the chance to develop enough confidence to speak publicly about issues overlooked by mainstream debate, and by providing forums in which it is possible to do so. The best of such work is able to act as a catalyst for lasting change rather than an isolated intervention. An interesting example in this respect remains Street Arts Community Theatre Company's work with a group of single mothers in Inala, outside of Brisbane, Australia. Following this intervention the group of mothers formed their own theatre group, Icy Tea, who continue to make work with the community. Examples such as this reveal the lasting effects that can stem from the best of community interventions.

Community theatre can take many different forms, from the Community Play (such as those produced by Ann Jellico) to Reminiscence Theatre (Banner, Word and Action, Age Exchange) in which participants make work based on their own memories. It can also range from professional theatre performed to a community on a community-based theme (researched with or without the aid of community members) to significant participation by the community members themselves. The earliest community theatres were relatively non-participatory: the first, set up by Peter Cheeseman at the Victoria Theatre in Stoke-on-Trent in 1962, had no playwright; nevertheless work was devised by the actors and directors with no participation or intervention by the community for which it was made. Even where community members are actively involved, the level to which the final product is considered important also varies enormously. At one extreme, devising companies performing to communities are, currently, increasingly expected to produce professional-quality productions, which may end up being either entertainment-driven or mere didacticism. At the other extreme are drama therapy and other therapeutic forms, whose *raison d'être* is the individual participant's well-being and mental health.

Generally speaking, however, community theatre developed over the 1980s and 1990s from making theatre *for* particular groups of people to making theatre *with* those groups. Much of this work was, in effect, a form of leisure activity, with its purpose the learning of a few basic skills and the provision, perhaps, of a pleasant evening out. The best of it was something more, having at its core the desire to explore ways of creating theatre that was meaningful, pertinent and engaging to those who had traditionally been excluded from participation. Whilst for many any 'accidental' qualities in performance were a mere by-product of the process, for some practitioners there was also a desire, and a challenge, to develop a practice whereby the creativity and concerns of the practitioner worked in conjunction with those of the participants. Here the high standards and personal and social benefits of the process might also be matched by similar achievements in performance.[12] If both process and product are perceived as being underpinned by the development of effective communication (in the workshop or rehearsal room, communication between the group; in the theatre, communication with an audience) then there need not be any essential contradiction between the two. Experience shows, however, that whilst most people are able to develop within the workshop/rehearsal room, a significantly smaller number of people are able to do so within the context of performing to a wider audience. This is to some extent related to audience expectation: what is truthfully, authentically and effectively communicated may not always be in line with the expectations of a less-than-open audience.

Drama therapy, psychodrama and other process-based therapeutic forms, such as those influenced directly or indirectly by Boal's 'Forum Theatre',[13] were able to avoid the potentially negative effect of audience expectation by providing instead an expressive outlet for dealing with personal issues. Through the use of role-play, drama could allow the participant to understand their own role within the family dynamic, for example, and be able to imagine other potential outcomes. In this way drama therapy enables the individual to step outside of the inauthentic roles that they may have found themselves playing in the 'drama of life'. Chris Johnston speaks of the ways in which community theatre can give 'energy to the quiet voices of those who have often been silent'.[14] He also notes however, against the prevalent view that the quality of dramatic material in therapeutic or community work remains unimportant, the way in which

> those coming to a devising process without formal training, can and often do make highly effective theatre ... They can project dramatic material effectively because they're less concerned with technical excellence than with whether or not that material is true to their own experience.[15]

Nevertheless the notion of judging such work remains anathema to most working in these areas, and for good reason: if a person is judged to be a 'poor performer' it will radically undermine that person's confidence and indeed their right to creative expression, both of which would be inappropriate within a strictly therapeutic context. This context also need not take into account the potentially conservative expectations of audiences, who may not perceive such work as 'effective theatre' regardless of its true value, and whose presence therefore in such a context is potentially undermining.

Just as some have questioned Boal for moving away from overt political issues to the 'personal is political' aspects of individual mental health, it does remain important to ensure, within this highly personalised emphasis, that the individual is enabled in each case to develop as a (creatively expressive) person. There is a danger, in therapeutic work, of simply encouraging the individual to conform better to society's expectations. This is an especially important question in relation to, for example, work with offenders, the unemployed or single mothers, since it may tend inadvertently to downplay the ways in which society itself produces offenders, lack of jobs and single mothers, so returning 'the political' to 'the personal'. Such work, in part due to funding issues and perhaps in part also due to the loss of belief in collective action and the rise of emphasis on personal empowerment in the wake of Conservative and New Labour policies, is now the most prevalent form of community art and theatre. It places the emphasis squarely on the individual's sense of self-esteem and is certainly valuable if it helps people to deal with painful emotions or to tackle difficult issues in their lives. Some community-focused theatre today, and particularly that of current TIE programmes (CragRats, Impact, *et al.*) is valuable but, arguably, a sanitised version of its forebears; the worst of it constitutes little more than animated manuals on personalised and emotive issues of interest to the community (e.g. Road Safety, Healthy Eating, Drugs). It nevertheless remains 'theatre with a message'.

The TIE movement was central to the emergence of the sort of community theatre that is now usually available for those with learning disabilities. TIE began in 1965 with the founding of the first British TIE team at the Belgrade Theatre in Coventry and emerged in part in response to new child-focused models of learning and the central importance to these of the notion of 'play'. Inspired by the Belgrade, and often borrowing its staff, many other TIE groups were set up at regional theatres between 1968 and 1970 and continued to be developed into the 1980s (Cockpit, Greenwich Young People's Theatre, Leeds TIE, and so on). Work was mostly devised and involved the children in direct interaction, usually involving some form of ethical, political or social issue being played out. Whilst the TIE companies were primarily interested in helping an audience to come to a better understanding of a subject, issue or concept, and while their politics were not nearly so overt as those of the early agitprop groups, their perceived political efficacy is revealed by Norman Tebbitt's attempt in the mid-eighties to have Theatre Centre banned from performing their play *Susumu's Story* in his constituency, with the issue even being raised in the House of Commons. Again, such groups are less politically overt now, where indeed they have managed to survive. Controversial content has been largely driven out by the National Curriculum and the current pressure on teachers to remain 'on message', as well as by a more general shift towards the notion of the individual rather than societal problems.

The ethics of community theatre have been discussed by, amongst others, Helen Nicholson, and echo those debates within community arts generally relating to the appropriateness of going into and then retreating from a community, and the assumptions that such work is inherently valuable and will necessarily have long-term effects. Even those whose work has been most influential in this area are aware of the hazards of such an approach – Ed Berman of Inter-Action admits, for example, that follow-up was relatively poor in the early days of the group. Naseem Khan's description of community art is also notable for the hint of cynicism it belies in relation to the possible differing perceptions of community work in the eyes of the community and of the practitioners: 'The use of different artists within a community to stimulate the participation of people in that particular art-form: usually – and mainly, in the minds of the practitioners – for some form of social improvement.'[16] It is also true that too many community projects that claim to translate the wishes of the participants result – in art and architecture interventions for example – in a physical object that few participants would actually have envisioned or indeed wished to see in their community. The intervening professional may end up, consciously or not, imposing their own vision by translating the community's ideas in ways that are alien to the participants. Thus the issue of how the participants' needs are actually translated and realised is crucial. In theatre at least the participants have a direct say in the content and verbal expression of any particular play.

Another potential difficulty with community theatre – and one that is relevant to the approaches we advocate in this book – is that it may tend to assume that the community's central interests are those of the community itself, in effect empowering communities to tell their stories regardless of whether these are what the community really wishes to discuss. Mainstream theatre, even when poorly produced or patronising in its content, does at least often presuppose an interest in issues and themes beyond the day-to-day realities of the theatre-going classes. Community theatre, in the fact that it is devised (either with or without the community) around issues specific to that community, may in fact foreclose the possibility of interest in issues *outside* of that community or within the wider world. We are not denying the importance of local interest and issues and it is true that these are the issues least likely to be tackled by mainstream debate or to receive a public hearing, which community theatre can provide; indeed, we have worked in these areas. The difficulty arises when members of a community would prefer to make work on themes or issues beyond those of the community itself. For those with learning disabilities, as we have already highlighted, the foreclosure of such a possibility may even amount to the assumption that they have little to say on matters not related to their disability. Furthermore in this case, since it is against the standards of those *without* learning disabilities that learning 'disability' is measured, the presence of a learning disability may in fact be more obviously apparent to those without one than to those to whom the label is ascribed. The work we advocate in this book instead provides a forum for actors with learning disabilities to express themselves creatively on any given theme.

Community work, finally, is by definition made for the community; it assumes by its very nature that whatever material is produced will be of only notional interest to those outside of the participating group. While advocacy and access work is crucial, in our own work we are concerned to avoid the potential 'ghettoisation' of actors with learning disabilities and the issues of concern to them, which may even serve to increase rather than decrease the distance between mainstream theatre-goers and those for whom such theatre has little appeal. Actors with learning disabilities, like all other actors, are interested in their own emotions and lives – and their lives amount to significantly more than their disabilities.

Theatre, Disability and Learning Disability

In the greater scheme of radical theatre, learning disability, then, was the last-comer, with the most politically active companies all but abandoned by the time learning disability was publicly acknowledged, and with the political impetus to bring theatre to the people now channelled for the most part into community and therapeutic work. Thus theatre's engagement with learning disability coincided with the beginnings of increased specialisation in target community groups, with government emphasis on being able to show proof of 'ameliorative effects', perhaps making specialist groups more obviously fruitful. Writing in 2006, Heddon and Milling describe a scenario in which, 'In recent years, funding criteria have led to an increased move towards specialisation in the target client groups in community work ... The growth of Boalean influence in this kind of community work is difficult to overemphasise.'[17]

Within the physical disability movement, however, a new awareness of differing subjectivities in the wider context of identity politics had led to the emergence of theatre groups whose primary aims were, firstly, to allow disabled people to make theatre and, secondly, to use this theatre as a forum for discussion about disability itself. Graeae Theatre was founded in 1980 by actor Nabil Shaban and director Richard Tomlinson, not only due to the fact that there was little visibility of disability issues in mainstream theatre but because, as Shaban notes, 'even local amateur dramatic societies at that time looked askance at having disabled people on stage'.[18] Graeae generated their plays through discussions by the group of disabled actors, which were then translated into scripts, as in *Sideshow* of 1980 and *3D* of 1981. As early as 1983 however, only three years after its formation, the founders had left and the company moved towards the performance of externally written work, echoing the general trend, in the 1980s and beyond, for collaborative work to drift back into mainstream divisions of labour.

Theatre groups with actors with learning disabilities have continued to work collaboratively, however. Mind the Gap is a professional theatre company, founded by Tim Wheeler and Susan Brown, who produce devised as well as script-led touring and local work with actors with learning disabilities, occasionally integrating non-disabled actors. They also run workshops and educational programmes, and have worked with Augusto Boal and his Forum Theatre methods on a number of occasions, exploring themes such as the accessibility of theatre to young people with learning disabilities. Their stated aim is to 'dismantle the barriers to artistic excellence so that learning disabled and non-disabled artists can perform alongside each other as equals'[19] and the issues explored by Mind the Gap, as well as its offshoot SFX Theatre Company, comprised of actors with learning disabilities, are specifically aimed at raising the profile of people with learning disabilities as professional theatre practitioners. Geraldine

Ling's work with The Lawnmowers, by contrast, has a less pragmatic and more overtly political agenda, with the work for the most part concerned with the politics of learning disability.

At the other extreme and, of necessity, eschewing overt political discussion, Oily Cart, based in London, make work for those with profound and multiple learning disabilities, touring to special schools and theatres across the UK. First Movement (based in Matlock and working predominantly in Derbyshire and Leicestershire) make performances over a longer timescale in which some of the performers themselves have profound and multiple learning disabilities. Concurrent with our own concerns and discoveries, Oily Cart have developed notions of 'multi-sensory' and non-linear narrative that combine sensory stimulation with the theatrical potential of non-verbal story-telling. Those with profound and multiple learning disabilities have in common a number of different forms of sensory deprivation: a visual impairment or a hearing difficulty; limited mobility and therefore an inability to reach out and touch things; sometimes a limited capacity to digest certain foods, thus depriving them of experiencing certain tastes. Compelled to produce work with which this audience can really engage, a director, in our own experience, is required to go 'back to basics', to think about how we experience the world on a fundamental level: the sensation of moving from dark into light or from a confined space to an open one, for example, or even how the 'energy' of an angry person is different to that of a loving person.[20] The context is specific and extreme, nevertheless the same impetus, the desire to speak to audiences in their own theatrical 'tongue' (and indeed to allow actors to speak in their own way), is also crucial to our general approach to working with actors with learning disabilities.

Different Equalities, Differing Subjectivities

For all other groups of society unique subjectivities have been proposed; new expressive languages have been proposed too. Yet for those with learning disabilities, both technical definitions and general impressions refer not to a form of *difference* but to a 'flaw', 'impairment' or 'defect' – in short a negative deviation from the 'norm'.

In the UK, the National Health Service simply describes learning disability as 'a condition that either prevents or hinders somebody from learning basic skills or acquiring information at the same rate as most people of the same age'.[21] The American Disabilities Education Act of 2004 is more precise in describing it as 'a disorder in one or more of the basic psychological processes involved in understanding or using language, spoken or written, that may manifest itself in an imperfect ability to listen, think, speak, read, write, spell or to do mathematical calculations.'[22]

Words such as 'hinders', 'condition', 'disorder' and – particularly provocative – 'imperfect' highlight the way in which those with learning disabilities are perceived to be *lacking*, rather than *different*. The disability movement's turn away from the individual model of disability (also known as the 'tragedy model') to the redefinition of physical disability as impairment and of disability rather as 'the social barriers, restrictions and/or oppressions they [those with physical disabilities] face'[23] remains useful in distinguishing between inherent difficulties and difficulties caused by society's expectations or refusals of acknowledgment. Similarly, whilst it may be true that having a learning disability creates problems for those who have them, it is debatable to what extent these problems are related to the learning disability, and to what extent to a society that 'thinks' and communicates in a certain way and that sees any deviation – intended or otherwise – as a fatal flaw.

In identity politics and in the general drive towards acceptance of difference from the 1960s and 1970s onwards it has been assumed that, despite being different to each other, people will all have equal access to verbal expression, if not to public acknowledgment of that expression. It has been assumed, too, that similar types of self-censorship have been produced under society's symbolic codes (albeit that these codes might be differently, and more rigorously, inflicted on black people than on white, or on women than on men, for example). Yet for those with learning disabilities these assumptions quite simply do not hold true, nor is a person with a learning disability ordinarily able to eloquently refute such assumptions through the usual verbal or written means. In fact when it comes to those with learning disabilities the notion that there is any kind of legitimate worldview or worldviews is barely acknowledged. Even if society has moved beyond the idea that people with learning disabilities have no inner life whatsoever, it nevertheless often fails to credit people with learning disabilities with the full range of emotions, imagination, physicality and sensations that so-called 'normal people' are able to experience. Crucially this also means that society fails to afford those with learning disabilities the possibility of growth and development in their lives.

And this worldview can be highly expressive – a language with inherent aesthetic and imaginative possibilities – which can be engaged with by those without disabilities if we are able to work together through observation, empathy and responsiveness, and through discovering more effective communication methods than verbal language alone. A lack of skill in verbal communication does not – a point we will purposefully reiterate throughout this book – amount to an inability to express oneself. Verbal expression is only one of many forms of expression and perhaps, in many ways, it is one of the least effective.

Theatre practitioners over the last thirty or so years have come together to create work that reflects their own expressive worldviews. Yet learning disability has always been the bridge too far for many in professional theatre, even within the world of disability arts where learning disability continues to be shunned – with one dance company, for example, refusing (not too long ago) to work with dancers with learning disabilities because they could not conform to the disciplines of a traditional approach to dance. Thus whilst issue-led and advocacy work continues to be crucial in tackling persistent and pressing social issues around access and perceptions, it nevertheless remains within a world of conceptual ideas that may be alien to the expressive *internal* world of the actor with learning disabilities. Rehearsals and post-performance or interactive discussions also still rely to some extent on verbal communication – a form of communication that, by definition, comes less naturally for those with learning disabilities. Issue-led work must continue, since general awareness of learning disability is still riddled with misconceptions. Yet a further theatre must be made, however, which enables actors with learning disabilities to forge a radically expressive theatrical form, a unique and legitimate theatrical language. This different vision in turn demands new definitions of quality and talent; it asks for the work to be judged – it even actively wants to be critiqued – yet it also asks that the work be engaged with and critiqued through criteria appropriate to its own aesthetic framework. We argue for the right for those with learning disabilities to practice professionally and the right to work towards a new aesthetic – even if that aesthetic requires a different set of criteria for assessing its quality. Crucial to this notion of a fitting aesthetic is the attendant notion of authenticity – for us the most essential criterion for a true dramatic experience. In the following chapter we locate our emphasis on authenticity within a broader search for authenticity in theatre over the twentieth century. Having done so, we begin to discuss how to make truly authentic theatre.

3. Brian Haigh, Kevin Dyson and Peter Wandtke in Knock Knock by Full Body and the Voice. © 2004 Patrick Fabre.

II
Authenticity

Most contemporary performance directors would agree that authenticity lies at the heart of what they wish to present to an audience, as well as to a large extent informing the choice of actors with whom they would seek to work. Whether the performance is a 'realist' theatrical presentation set in a particular historical timeframe and utilising traditional costume, or a non-realist work set in a fantastical future – or, indeed, in no 'naturalistic' timeframe at all – the performance still has to 'ring true'. Can the audience believe in it? Is the audience engaged? Do we recognise the relationships between the performers – or between the solo performer and their environment? Can we empathise with the emotions presented, whether through the spoken word or physical movement? Or does the performance strike us as wooden, lacking in chemistry, lacking in integrity? Even where the work sets out to puncture the notion of realism, or where empathising too readily with the performers is perceived as politically problematic,[1] a certain believability surely remains essential in order to ensure the viewer's engagement. Quite simply, without a measure of authenticity, understood in its widest sense, the spectator is liable to vacate the performance – if not physically, then emotionally.

This was not always the case, however; indeed in some mainstream theatre today authenticity on the part of the actors still seems low on the agenda. In traditional voice-based training, of course, a certain theatricality has been prized, especially in traditional renditions of Shakespeare, for example. With the widespread shift to 'method acting' and the close-ups and prolonged silences of film and television, as well as the dismantling of traditional theatre forms outlined in the previous chapter, this sort of overt theatrical rhetoric has been for the most part undermined. Both television and film's physical formats require a subtlety in the small gesture that the stage may not demand – in film in particular a facial expression, magnified on a large cinema screen, can seem absurd if the acting is overt. The best stage directors also strive to avoid the overtly theatrical, with 'authenticity' ever more prized as essential to the true dramatic experience.

Authenticity is, for us, the very underpinning of good theatre and is also therefore the most important attribute we look for, and seek to develop, in a potential actor. This is the case regardless of the actors we work with. Yet if authentic behaviour is widely held to be covered over by imposed ideologies and social codes, and since learning disability is generally perceived as a 'failure' to fully assimilate these social codes, then the question of authenticity is of particular relevance.

The Quest for Authenticity

Philosophers have long strived to ascertain how much of human nature is inherent and how much learned. Rousseau, writing in the eighteenth century, had already posed the question of what constitutes the 'natural condition' of the human being and authors such as Castiglione, writing on court manners during the Renaissance, have recorded the ways in which our behaviour is governed by social rules. This concern came to the fore in the twentieth century, with both artists and scientists setting out to uncover the layers of repression and socialisation inherent to the 'human condition'.

The quest for authenticity in theatre is part of this wider quest to unearth the remnants of authentic behaviour beneath the strata of social and psychological impositions. At the heart of this search lies the deeper question of what authenticity is or, differently put, how authentic 'authenticity' can be achieved. Whilst the nature of human behaviour and development is beyond the scope of this book, it is clear that for all 'socialised' beings, a complex array of codes, behaviours and etiquettes make completely uncensored behaviour impossible if we are to survive in the world. Even the most unsociable and spontaneous of us would be hard put to claim that our behaviour is entirely unmediated.

There are numerous histories of and theories about the nature of the socialised self, ranging from those dealing primarily with our conscious social behaviours to those, such as the work of Judith Butler, that argue that gender itself is a repeated cultural performance. The most fundamental shift in thinking in the twentieth century was perhaps that introduced by psychoanalysis, with its 'founder' Sigmund Freud uncovering an entire substratum of unconscious impulses that make problematic the notion of complete control and, indeed, complete authenticity.[2]

The crucial difference between Freud's work and that of earlier writers on social behaviour lies in the notion of consciousness – we might think we are consciously controlling our behaviour and self-image, even if, due to rigid social coding, we have little choice in the matter. For Freud much of our repression is not only out of our control but entirely unknown to us. Whilst it would be a stretch to suggest that Freud's theory of the unconscious has driven the changes in Western theatre practice in the last century, it certainly influenced those who, early in the century, set out to expose the extent to which accepted social codes – which many took to be natural – were in fact imposed through society's demands. This was especially the case for those seeking to overturn the 'bourgeois' order from whom all of Freud's patients were drawn.

Perhaps of all thinkers or movements the Surrealists, active in the early to mid-twentieth century, were most dedicated to exposing the ideologically imposed nature of the mediated self. Surrealism set out to lay bare and indeed overturn the hypocrisy of bourgeois thinking through the release of the unconscious. Influenced by Freud's work, as well as founder André Breton's own experiences working with war-trauma victims in the Paris asylums, the Surrealists employed various methods of tapping into supposedly unfiltered authentic unconscious thought, including 'automatic writing' and the recording of dreams (for Freud, the 'royal road' to the unconscious). Despite the criticisms levelled at the movement (for many, the movement maintained traditional gender roles even as it sought to undermine them), Surrealism remains a uniquely wholehearted and influential attempt to expose the machinations of ideology and socialisation on the human mind.

The difficulty for Surrealism was the difficulty faced by anybody seeking to grasp the nature of 'total authenticity'. Notwithstanding its important insights on the maltreatment of the insane, the movement perhaps failed to fully acknowledge the conundrum at its core: that complete de-socialisation results in debilitating mental illness; that a certain amount of 'inauthenticity' – and containment – is in fact necessary. As such Surrealism, when taken to its ultimate conclusion, could only be fully integrated by those whose ability to live 'in reality' was already highly precarious – this is why Breton's 'Nadja',[3] apparently already on the verge of a breakdown when he met her, was perhaps the ultimate Surrealist muse. Many in the movement suffered mental health problems; Breton himself seems to have kept his own psychological barriers very much intact, however, and as such his own search for authenticity contained a fundamental contradiction.

For others the search for the authentic self and the discovery of basic human 'drives' was undertaken in direct relation to theatre. Already in 1872 Friedrich Nietzsche, in *The Birth of Tragedy*,[4] had in relation to Greek tragedy set out his idea of two contrasting but complementary drives: the Dionysian and the Apollonian. Nietzsche's Dionysian drive, despite being formulated previous to Freud's notion of libido, does seem to suggest a similar innate and inchoate drive which, in splitting into forms, symbols and images through the Apollonian drive towards image-making, becomes contained (or even sublimated, to map onto Nietzsche a Freudian term) in images. Nietzsche seems to have sensed the importance of a balance between the two: the Dionysian drive alone, in its uncontained and frenzied state, is barely imaginable. Whilst the Surrealists certainly made images – at first through words and photographs and, later, paintings – they were perhaps more interested in the release of drives than in their subsequent containment.

The French actor Antonin Artaud, briefly a member of the Surrealist movement but later expelled on political grounds, also sought to release a deeply buried impulse. Artaud's influence on twentieth-century Western theatre practice has been as extensive as it is difficult to pinpoint in any pragmatic sense: Peter Brook succinctly notes that 'Artaud applied is Artaud betrayed'.[5] Artaud's deeply held desire was to rescue theatre from the dry, escapist entertainment it had become and to return it to a powerful, almost sacred, pre-verbal impulse. Critic André Green, writing in 1979, saw Artaud's work as another attempt to lift the repression of socialisation.[6] For Artaud, the essence or 'origin' of drama is less specific even than the primal ritual: it should be 'a secret psychic impulse, speech prior to words';[7] 'strange signs matching some dark prodigious reality we have repressed once and for all here in the West'.[8]

Though he does not quite use this terminology, Artaud, like the Surrealists, seems to argue for the release of the unconscious or, as Nietzsche might have it, the frenzied Dionysian drive; nor does he counter the intoxicated Dionysian with the Apollonian drive towards meaning and image-making – this is perhaps why Artaud's 'theatre' seems impossible to actually visualise, let alone, as Brook has noted, perform. Artaud's exact meaning remains perhaps necessarily vague. What is clear is that this 'dark prodigious reality' is so deeply buried, so authentic, that we can barely imagine it. Despite the lack of precision and ultimate impracticability – perhaps even because of it – Artaud's desire to rescue theatre from its role as bourgeois entertainment has been influential for many attempting to rejuvenate theatre in the twentieth and twenty-first centuries. Crucially – and certainly in this sense relevant to our interests – Artaud's 'reality' is beyond or prior to the spoken word. As such he remains an important precursor to the devised and physical theatre movements. His ideas highlight the way in which the 'tyranny of words' betrays a deeper, more immediate reality. Overturning this 'tyranny' is crucial to the work discussed in this book and is therefore a theme to which we shall return.

Less extreme but just as important was the influence of the Russian director Constantin Stanislavski, also working in the early twentieth century. Stanislavski's 'Method', which was taught as commonplace in drama schools by at least the mid-century, asks the actor to delve more deeply into the psychological motivations of the character. It was in part the widespread acceptance of 'method acting' that led to a generation of actors who desired a deeper involvement with the entire theatrical process and, along with the wider political shifts that we have outlined, eventually contributed to the development of devised rather than traditional script-led theatre. Method acting certainly stresses authenticity, yet even here the psychological motives remain those of an imposed and already existing character, pre-considered by a scriptwriter and or/director. Each actor might 'shade' this character differently, yet the actor's own psychology is still to some extent left at the door. The actor might draw on their own experience of, for example, loss or pain in order to access the requisite tears or distress, yet this is always at the service of the role to which these tears are proffered.

For many directors and practitioners the 'Method' still stops short of true authenticity. Indeed for Bertolt Brecht, a rare critic of Stanislavski, the whole notion of merging actor and character was problematic, since it covered over and naturalised the constructed nature of the character and the attendant ideologies or worldviews that such pre-formed characters inevitably put forward. Others have attempted to go beyond the notion of drawing on 'reality' in the service of a role to reach greater levels of authenticity and also to forge a deeper connection between actor and character. In his 'Statement of Principles' Polish director Jerzy Grotowski, himself influenced by the work of Stanislavski, as well as that of Meyerhold, addressed the tension between the cerebral aspects of acting and the 'liberated authentic state':

> The rhythm of life in modern civilization is characterized by pace, tension, a feeling of doom, the wish to hide our personal motives and the assumption of a variety of roles and masks in life ... We like to be 'scientific', by which we mean discursive and cerebral, since this attitude is dictated by the course of civilization ... we play a double game of intellect and instinct, thought and emotion; we try to divide ourselves artificially into body and soul.[9]

Grotowski, whose aim was through theatre to rediscover the 'human essence beneath the influence of culture',[10] does appear to assume that such a division were a personal choice, and also seems to perceive this state of affairs as a contemporary condition. In fact the 'game' of socialisation is ongoing; the very process of socialisation demands such a division of us, as we have seen in relation to Surrealism. To eliminate completely 'the time-lapse between inner impulse and outer reaction',[11] as Grotowski advocates, would require levels of un-learning that may be all but impossible. Grotowski's basic aim is nevertheless shared by many – and here we include ourselves – who perceive authenticity as a fundamental premise for profound theatre.

For other practitioners authenticity has had a rather different meaning, with the focus on the spectator rather than the actor. Here the emphasis is on the importance of the spectator's authentic action in the world, on his or her ability to consciously transcend imposed ideologies and political regimes. As such this approach is more overtly politically driven, concerned with the external impact of politics rather than the ideologies assimilated unconsciously by the individual. It was the Brazilian director Augusto Boal who made an overt link between theatre and the actual social and political circumstances of both the actors and audiences, and also emphasised the need to break down the distinction *between* the actor and the audience. Boal's stance, as we have noted, was echoed by those, discussed in the previous chapter, who endeavoured to allow the audience increased participation in the performance event.

Boal challenged the efficacy of the classical notion of catharsis put forward by Aristotle: the theatrical experience might well produce a sudden release of emotion but, for Boal, it nevertheless left the spectator essentially unchanged. Instead it is crucial that the spectator (transformed into the spect-actor) actually participates, since vicariously living the experience represented on stage only reduces the spectator's capacity for action. In fact Boal's stance has altered since the ideas set out in his enormously influential *Theatre of the Oppressed*.[12] In later years his thinking has moved towards a more psychological model of repression, replacing his notion of the 'cop in the street' with that of 'the cop in the head'. This stance sees the function of theatre as more subtly influencing the participant's experience of life and the ways in which he or she interacts in the world, rather than propelling the actor into direct action. It is this later work that has received some criticism by those whose concern remains with external political events – this is understandable in particularly brutal political climates. In Europe, however, Boal's later work continues to be an enormous influence on applied and community theatre.

Dialogue, interaction and the accessibility of theatre are also central to the rather more playful and less politicised approaches of Clive Barker and to those, such as Chris Johnston, who continued to develop his ethos and methods. The quest for authenticity has been to a large extent the impetus for the devised work discussed in the previous chapter, particularly that 'visual theatre' or 'performance art theatre' which stemmed from an art or crossover art–theatre background and which emphasised 'action' and 'liveness'. As Heddon and Milling note:

> the liveness of performance led often to a focus on action rather than on acting, and performing equated with doing rather than pretending. Perhaps paradoxically, live performance offered the potential for authentic activity and within this frame, representation might best be reconsidered as presentation.[13]

Crucially, such theatre seeks to go beyond the limiting impositions of scripted characters. It also retains Artaud's belief in a realm of experience which lies beneath – or beyond – words.

Total authenticity, understood as completely unmediated 'animal' behaviour, is impossible for the adult human if we are not to slip into complete psychosis or to be rejected completely by society. Nevertheless the level to which a person is enslaved by mediated behaviours and imposed ideologies varies greatly – for some, unquestioned assimilation into rigidly prescribed roles can become the source of psychological pain; drama therapy and psychodrama have understood the power of theatre to redress the more damaging aspects of socialisation. It is these aspects of the socialisation process that we are also interested in overcoming, though our motivations differ. Despite the inherent limitations, authenticity – and especially an authenticity that lies behind the veil of words – remains central to our approach to theatre-making. Having located our discussion with the wider framework of the search for authenticity in theatre, we want now to look more specifically at the implications of the notion of authenticity for the work made by actors with learning disabilities.

Learning Disability, Authenticity and Socialisation

In theatrical terms there are a number of factors that are generally understood to contribute to a sense of authenticity: a lack of self-consciousness on the performers' part; a lack of overt technique; a sense of being truly in the moment. Since learning disability is frequently defined precisely as a *lack* of sophistication in social skills, which rely on self-consciousness, social technique and an awareness of being observed by others, there may be a sense in which, for an actor with a learning disability, authenticity is in fact the more 'natural' stance. We must be careful not to make sweeping assumptions – by suggesting for example that those with learning disabilities are always inevitably 'authentic' in their behaviour and interactions. Yet perhaps our reticence to confront such issues has also served to suppress certain important elements of the differing 'worldview' of those with learning disabilities. In the desire to be 'inclusive' we run the risk of failing to acknowledge particular qualities inherent to the nature of learning disability that may in fact be powerfully employed in theatrical performance.

Learning disability is ordinarily taken to refer to a 'failure' or 'lack' of full socialisation, in terms, officially, of a failure to grasp basic symbolic necessities of communication – reading, writing, verbal communication and so forth – and, unofficially, of a failure to know how and when to 'censor' certain 'inappropriate' behaviours. Increasingly, and in line with the disability movement's emphasis on speaking one's own story, those with impairments that do not affect writing and speaking are engaged in telling their own histories. A person with Asperger's Syndrome, for example, may never quite grasp the complex codes of social behaviour, frequently finding themselves embarrassed – or the source of embarrassment – for having seemingly 'refused' to follow the rule (in fact, not understood) that it is inappropriate to ask personal question of strangers, or to simply walk off when a conversation bores us. This does not prevent people with Asperger's Syndrome, however, from describing the situation from their own point of view, a point of view from which these social codes may seem impossible, illogical or even dishonest. Amongst others Temple Grandin and Naseem Khan, both autistic, have also written very eloquent books about their disabilities.

For many people with a learning disability to eloquently write or verbalise his or her own viewpoint is impossible by the very nature of the disability. This does not curtail the possibility of such a person expressing their viewpoint through non-verbal means, however. If theatre is one such expressive vehicle then it is clear from our experience that a crucial difference between the 'worldview' of the person with a learning disability and that of the non-disabled person relates to the levels of assimilation of imposed self-censorship. Whilst certainly still present (and sometimes even aggravated by low self-esteem), this censorship is often less fully developed in the armoury of social tools for those with learning disabilities than for those without. The developments in identity politics outlined in the previous chapter exposed the fact that 'normality' is a construction and is better understood (in the current terminology) as 'normativity', that is, the imposition of standards of normality by the dominant group. Quite simply, excellent social performance is not 'normal' for the person with a learning disability. As such, the lack of highly sophisticated and fully assimilated social behaviours will naturally tend to produce a more (though not, of necessity, completely) authentic mode of engagement with performance practices. By contrast, for those who do have full access to the skills necessary to follow the rules, etiquette, mores and codes of the 'socialised world', authenticity may be especially difficult to attain, depending on what we understand as being authentic in the first place. Furthermore when the actor with a learning disability produces theatre in a manner that is authentic to them, this differing worldview and manner is also *authenticated* and made available to the wider culture as a valid and viable means of expression. This is, crucially, a political act.

In fact actors with learning disabilities who are just starting out *do* bring inauthentic behaviours into the rehearsal room. As with anyone new to acting but with an inclination towards drama, many aspiring actors who have a learning disability bring with them preconceived notions of theatre. They may have a limited diet of acting based on pantomime and soap opera and can bring curious forms of 'pastiche acting' into the studio. Most directors working with non-professionals in community theatre will have also come across this scenario, and even trained actors have been known to produce the same effect, that of performing the notion of 'performance'. We see this whenever we find ourselves remarking on 'what a wonderful actor' somebody is: surely here we are noticing an overt performance style that makes true authenticity impossible.

A great deal of the early 'inauthenticity' of the actor with a learning disability derives from having learned behaviours in response to a world that has denied his or her validity as a fully socialised human being, without necessarily having assimilated the reasons why he or she 'ought' to behave in this way. We have all learned to adapt our behaviours in response to others. To an extent this is healthy; beyond a certain point it becomes destructive, as we have seen. Perhaps the crucial difference lies in the fact that, for most of us, we have at least a vague understanding of *why* we are expected to behave in a particular way, even if we do not necessarily agree with its premise. We have at least a level of self-consciousness about our 'role'.[14] More cynically put, perhaps, those of us without learning disabilities are rather more aware of what we stand to gain in signing the social contract. For these reasons, once a person with a learning disability begins to dismantle these inauthentic behaviours, they may in fact have less to battle with than others. Their self-censorship will have less conceptual validity (they will not, for instance, tend to sit and weigh up the pros and cons of 'fitting in' with society's expectations), nor will the social masquerade be as sophisticated – and therefore ingrained – as it is for other people.

Embodied Performance: Actor and Role

For feminist and postcolonial theatre practitioners and artists working in the 1960s and beyond, the notion of embodiment was a reaction against the dualistic split between the mind and body (attributed to the philosopher Descartes, though hardly to his views alone) and an acknowledgment that our experience in the world is fundamentally affected by the bodies we inhabit, whether these be female bodies, male bodies, white or coloured bodies, 'able' or 'disabled bodies'. Our perception of the world, our way of inhabiting space and our subjectivity were seen to be inextricable from the bodies we inhabit, a fact made clear by phenomenologists such as Maurice Merleau-Ponty, who emphasised the place of our bodies in perception and did away with the idea of the 'disembodied' Cartesian mind. With the development of performance art and the feminist notion of the 'personal as political', a form of performance began to be imagined that could draw directly on the embodied personal experiences of the performer.

In the search for authentic performance over the twentieth century we see a gradual breakdown of the distinction between actor and character. Stanislavski's 'Method' was one such breakdown, and others such as Boal have also endeavoured to break down the distinction between actor and spectator. For us, the engagement between actor and spectator need not to be actual or physical; what is crucial is that the performance affects the spectator not by re-creating a 'moving scenario' but by pushing the spectator beyond his or her expectations into a place in which true engagement is possible. For this, authenticity on the part of the performers is essential, and the breakdown of the rigid lines between performer and character is a crucial aspect of this authenticity. Referring to the work of Forced Entertainment in their book *Devised Theatre*, Heddon and Milling note that:

> it is often difficult to determine fact or reality from fiction, actor from character, acting from non-acting. Actors often appear to shift between 'being themselves' and 'acting', with this shift perhaps revealing the act of acting, letting us witness the actors simply 'doing a job in front of another group of people'.[15]

They also speak of the way in which in devised performance, as well as in the Happenings of the 1960s, 'performers purport to present only themselves'.[16] Whilst this does not always lead to success (Brook writes of 'the sadness of a bad Happening' which 'unavoidably ... reflects the level of its inventor'),[17] the point is that in such work the line between authenticity and performance begins to blur. The same blurring of boundaries is found in the work of the legendary Living Theatre, the People Show and of The Theatre of Mistakes, whose aim was that of 'extending their own behaviour into the arena of the action presented to the public'.[18] The repetitive task-based elements of the Theatre of Mistakes, founded in 1974 by a poet and ex-dancer, one of a number of theatre groups whose work brushed up against contemporaneous interests in performance art, can hardly be called performances in the traditional sense. The 'actors' are focused on doing their allotted tasks, rather than on pretending to be someone or do something else, and such tasks for the most part were also workaday. In this blurring of art and life we again see the desire for authenticity: this is where 'acting' becomes 'action' and representation simply presentation.

An actor with a learning disability may not be able to separate discreetly the performed role from their own person and emotions at the moment of performance. This does not mean that the staged scenario is not a performance, nor does it mean that the actor is not aware of the fact of performing to an audience. Furthermore this 'lack of ability' is not a lack at all; indeed, as we have described, the ability to successfully merge actor and role is one that most practitioners working outside of the mainstream have been actively seeking throughout the twentieth century. Such a mode of performance, in which the boundaries between actor and role are permeable, may come closer to the notion of the 'performative' than that of the performance as traditionally understood – the term is complex and is used in various ways; what it tends to highlight is the idea of performance not as a re-presentation but as an act that in itself constitutes its own reality through being performed.[19] Nevertheless the idea of 'performing authentically' might seem curious, if performance is taken to imply some level of conscious awareness of an audience. What do we mean then by an 'authentic performance'?

We would argue that for an authentic act to be legitimately considered performance, the performer must remain consciously aware of the fact that he or she is performing *to someone else*, that is, that he or she is communicating to a spectator. This was highlighted during a recent visit to the theatre, which was interrupted by a member of the audience's mobile phone ringing during the most important soliloquy of the play. The performing actor was visibly disturbed: it was, in fact, the most authentic and theatrical moment in a fairly conventional performance. Yet we could not call it 'performance' per se. When we are engaged entirely in our own world – perhaps the ultimate form of authenticity, although in adulthood all our actions are mediated by an inner voice of approval, an internal spectator – we run the risk of alienating the audience through self-indulgence. Peter Brook has referred to this dilemma:

> It is hard to understand the true function of the spectator, there and not there, ignored and yet needed. The actor's work is never for an audience, yet always is for one. The onlooker is a partner who must be forgotten and still constantly kept in mind.[20]

Yet there are levels of performance and, as we have noted, levels of authenticity. If 'method acting' utilises some elements of the actor's own experience in the service of a role, it nevertheless runs the risk of reproducing the actor's own external (and inauthentic) observations. Brook speaks of the method actor

> reaching inside himself for an alphabet that is also fossilized, for the language of signs from life that he knows is the language not of invention but of his conditioning. His observations of behaviour are often observations of projections of himself. What he thinks to be spontaneous is filtered and monitored many times over.[21]

This points again to the notion that even in everyday life our responses and 'authenticity' are in effect already mediated by our conditioning. For an actor with a learning disability, it may be more difficult to draw a clear line between actor and character, self and role and, as well, to 'hide' or 'mediate' natural responses. Such a performance is neither completely real nor completely false, neither strictly a performance of character nor strictly an expression of the actor. If equality for us amounts to equality of access to theatrical vision, then the blurred line between 'real' and 'performed' that so many have sought is also very much a part of the theatrical vision of the actor with a learning disability. Rachel Karafistan, working with one of the authors' companies, has spoken of the way in which the actors

> seemed to have the ability to straddle the border between reality and imagination more effectively and honestly than 'ordinary' actors. I was fearful … at how far down they would voluntarily reach inside themselves (it usually takes 'ordinary' actors a lifetime of chipping away at their inhibitions to reach such truth.) … On the whole, actors with learning disabilities appear more able to negate their ego and as a result portray real truth.[22]

Authenticity in performance is not the same as unmediated spontaneity. Rather it is an entire approach to making theatre; it is as much in the intention as it is in the act. An actor may be well aware of performing on stage and to an audience, yet still be able to reach inside and engage with the audience in an authentic way. This hybrid understanding of performance – one which is neither oblivious to an audience nor re-constructed and re-presented from some external model – is highlighted in the fact that an engaged and authentic act may be repeated night after night without losing its authenticity. This may even mean that the performance changes subtly as the actor 'grows' into the role through the course of a play. If instead the actor finds that he or she is recreating the previous night's performance, losing the connection with themselves or with the audience, posing in or replicating the role, authenticity is lost.

In a piece directed by one of the authors, a scene involved a sedate woman in her late fifties, smartly dressed and moving slightly awkwardly, who approaches an inflatable chair.[23] The actor kicks out her foot and the chair shifts a couple of feet across the stage. Two musicians play a grand piano, one using the keys, the other hitting the strings with a drum stick inside the open lid. The sound reverberates around the auditorium; a stark white shaft of light illuminates the chair from above. Now the silhouetted figure begins to hit the chair with her fists, grunting with the effort of each blow. Three others join her and the chair is ravaged and beaten. A calm at last pervades the space. One of the piano players begins a mournful wailing. The performers have stepped back from the chair, staring at it, now deflated. Slowly they place their hands under it, lifting the chair above the shoulders. The wailing grows silent and the lights fade. The audience is left palpably shocked, disturbed, exhilarated. What is the nature of authenticity in this piece?

The woman has a learning disability and visual impairment, which cause her to move awkwardly. Her actions here are not choreographed (nor are those of the pianists) and the other actors join her only when it feels right to them. These actions are also quite out of character for the actor in the role. The energy and frustration expended in the beating of the chair is quite real; the same anger or aggression might have been emitted during a drama therapy session – yet the scene is repeated in every performance. The actor is well aware of the nature of the public performance; that she is involved in a conscious act of making theatre. She may or may not be aware of the 'clumsiness' of her movements as perceived by the audience – or at least, she may be aware on a bodily or intuitive rather than intellectual or verbalised level. What she certainly knows is that in this act she is able to reveal to the audience an aspect of herself that they do not expect to encounter. The scene has a double purpose however; it is also part of a wider work and may be perceived differently by the audience, who may also be more overtly aware of the 'difference' of the actor's bodily manner.

Many directors, working in both film and theatre, will be aware of subtle differences between the perceptions of the actor and the audience, and it is part of a director's job to mediate between the two. Some, such as Ken Loach, consciously direct actors to produce effects that may not be perceived by the actors themselves, and any screen test will reveal charismatic or interesting elements of a potential actor or performer that may not be apparent to the person being filmed. Nevertheless, with actors with learning disabilities, who may be unable directly to verbalise their own opinion of a piece or even to articulate in the usual way their understandings of the audiences' possible perceptions, the director has to be doubly aware of issues of trust, judgment, sensitivity and integrity – themes that run through this book for this reason. Actors can never be aware of the impact of every gesture they make; authenticity would be impossible if they tried. Furthermore if the director of actors with learning disabilities fails to trust him or herself, the end result may be tame or overly sensitive – in this sense patronising – and result in a form of false 'authenticity' that shirks from the rather scarier aspects of true authenticity. How does the director choose when and how to intervene in 'inappropriate' behaviour on stage? How does he or she know how to sensitively frame a scene? These are also questions to which we shall return.

In order to maintain authenticity – and indeed trust – the director must facilitate the actor's ownership of the work, even, or especially, where the actor is unable to articulate issues of possible audience perception. It is the director's role not only to aid the actor in reaching into themselves such that they are able to produce the performance but also to enable them to become increasingly aware of themselves and their own movements. The director must be able to open up the actor and also to challenge that actor to grow. Authenticity is rarely a quality that is always present but is one that can be developed in the actor: in the rehearsal room this might be achieved through various exercises such as eye contact, trust and touching exercises and expression, release and the eradication of emotional blocks, all of which require strong rapport, and integrity on the part of the director. What unsettles the boundaries of the performance described above and makes it more than simply a 'release of emotion' is the extent to which the actor is able to both feel and allow the aggression and the extent to which the performance draws on the actor's own reality (the awkwardness, the latent anger) without using these in the service of an externally imposed character, at the same time as also remaining aware of the spectator who 'must be forgotten and still constantly kept in mind'.

Without a clear awareness of the nature of their part in a performance, such work would be difficult to define as performance per se – sudden unexpected outbursts of anger are frequently 'theatrical', especially in an inappropriate setting, yet we would be hard pressed to refer to these as conscious performances. It also balances the Dionysian impulse with the Apollonian 'image'. It is not enough for the emotion to simply be released – it must also be expressed and communicated effectively. If the angry woman had her back to the audience, for example, or was not on some essential level sharing her feelings, there would be a sense in which the spectator was not supposed to be party to the event. What we witness in this scene is not complete spontaneity, nor is it a representation of an emotion or character. Instead it is a fully 'embodied' performance.

Peter Brook has noted the impossibility of conveying any theatrical meaning or import when movement is entirely absent. At the same time there are physical performances which, whilst clearly reliant on the body, do not necessarily reveal very much about the performer. In classical ballet, for example, the body is trained and honed as a tool in the service of abstract movements that form a particular 'language' and are rarely considered to be 'natural'. The dancer Darcey Bussell has spoken of the fact that her first performance of *Song of the Earth* was her first experience of embodying a role such that she forgot about the audience. The experience, for Bussell, was rare, and Bussell is herself a rare performer who is perhaps able to access a certain level of authenticity even within a seemingly abstract bodily language (which, having employed it for so long, may in fact now be 'natural' to her; *Song of the Earth* was also written especially for her by Kenneth MacMillan, who was already familiar with Bussell's particular style). Yet for many dancers such authenticity is unattainable and will in any case always be 'contained' or constrained within the language of the form. Our own physical work does not rely on skill-based, abstract movement and is instead intimately tied into the actor's own natural bodily manners and means of expression. For feminists, queer theorists and thinkers on race, embodiment goes far beyond the ability to 'feel' oneself caught up in a series of movements; instead the body we inhabit is profoundly caught up in our experience of the world: it also profoundly affects the way that body authentically 'performs'. Much work has been done by disabled writers, advocates and actors on the disabled body, too, and the way in which this body will bring to theatrical work its own particular condition and existence.

As we noted in Chapter I, the subjectivity of those with learning disabilities – perceived as different rather than 'flawed' - has perhaps been ignored quite simply because with all other 'differences' (race, class, gender, disabled or able-bodied) a certain communality of thought-capacity has been assumed as standard. Subjectivity has been gendered, raced, 'queered' and 'classed', with French feminists even arguing for the value of non-linear, non-logical thinking in the face of 'male rationality' – and indeed receiving opprobrium for some time from British and American feminists for this 'essentialism'. Yet in all cases a certain 'standard' in relation to skills such as 'understanding or using language, spoken or written', the 'ability to listen, think, speak, read, write, spell or use mathematical calculations'[24] has been assumed and, therefore, even implied as the basic criteria for subjectivity. The feminist writer, working in a non-linear or experimental manner, has the capacity to choose, in the first instance, to pursue this form. This 'option' to consciously subvert the 'norm' has been assumed to be openly available for expressive use. In emphasising the importance of differing bodies but assuming a commonality of thought processes perceived as basic, we might even say that such thinking has accidentally replicated the dualistic mind–body model against which it has supposedly fought.

How then is learning disability embodied, and how does such an embodiment manifest itself in theatre? How would the audience reaction have been different, in the scene described, had it been choreographed in more detail? If the woman was sleeker and more sure in her movements, could she then have faked – or performed – a clumsy stance in order to heighten the impact of the scene? Would this 'faking' have been spotted by the audience? The learning disabilities of the actor in this case were not particularly visible, unlike in the case of an actor with Down Syndrome, for example, whose appearance brings with it obvious signifiers of 'difference'. Yet, possibly due to a deep-rooted lack of confidence, as well as the slight visual impairment, her demeanour has a vulnerable quality. The audience then may sense something different or 'unusual' that they cannot quite put their finger on. In turn this difference will highlight a particular and individual form of embodied expression that is unique to the actor. The audience's awareness of and acceptance of the awkwardness of the actor is crucial if we are to claim honestly that we accept different types of (non-normative) bodies and bodily movements.

Yet, as we have argued, learning disability is perhaps the last frontier when it comes to the acceptance of difference and in any case the visible 'signs' of learning disability may be either overt in the case of Down Syndrome or only just perceptible. It may even be argued that the added theatrical impact of this awkwardness played on the woman's disability. To take such a stance would be in effect to misunderstand the notion of equality of access to vision in which we are interested, and also to censor which styles or natural physical attributes should be 'available' for theatre. If an actor has natural (untrained) grace, this grace will be allowed as a valid point of interest in a performance or screen test; for the same reasons natural clumsiness – the actor's 'true' physical manner – must equally be allowed into the performance and even noted as bringing something extra to it. The same might occur if any actor were asked to perform something which, for them, was particularly tricky – asking someone to walk a tightrope, for example, when they have never done so before. Clearly, it would be absurd to suggest that, for maximum theatrical impact, 'clumsy' actors must necessarily be engaged in similarly aggressive theatrical scenes, or that actors must always be asked to do something which, for them, is particularly difficult. In such cases the director would be actively imposing a difficult task with the express aim of heightening the 'spectacle' of the work for the audience; in the case of the actor with naturally awkward movements, such 'awkwardness' is part of her embodied day-to-day experience of the world.

This is a highly sensitive area, of course. How can we be certain as to how the actor perceives what they are portraying on stage? Whilst we can posit that no actor ever knows exactly what effect they are having, particularly if the director has a heavy directorial stance, it is entirely possible for the actor to fully 'get' the director's perception. This is most easily understood in film – whilst the film actor may not have a full understanding of the overall work and their part in it, he or she can later watch the film and perceive the way in which the director has employed or even manipulated their role (and may even object to it). By contrast if an actor with a learning disability watched a film in which he or she had in fact been manipulated or exploited the actor would not necessarily perceive this exploitation, even in retrospect, or might sense something awry but not be able to articulate it, even to themselves. (That is to say, he or she might 'know' intuitively, but not consciously, that exploitation has taken place). This raises crucial questions about our understanding of knowledge and self-consciousness. If someone *knows* something but does not 'know that they know' (i.e. self-consciously), how can we even speak of what that person knows? Again, words and conceptual understanding fail us – we must instead rely to a large extent on 'intuition' and 'sensing'. This highlights again quite how crucial are the roles of trust and integrity in the relationship between actor and director.

Whilst our work is not overtly political, it does have in common with overtly issue-led drama the fact that such 'issues' – for instance alcoholism or mental illness – are overloaded with symbolic short-hands, gestures, codings or 'signifiers of difference', which for many audiences have to be broken down in order for real understanding to emerge. We all know the stock motifs used to trigger rapidly the stereotypes of 'madness' (babbling, hand-wringing) or 'breakdown' or 'emerging alcoholism' (hand-rubbing, hair-tearing, twitching, darting eyes and so forth). Yet perhaps we are not so aware of the ways in which depictions of learning disability, rare as they are, frequently rely on certain 'signifiers of difference' and especially because, unlike physical disability, learning disability – except in the case of Down Syndrome – has no obvious physical 'signs'. One TV drama involving a character with a learning disability 'signalled' his difference (in this example conceived as comic stupidity) by having him, in the first scene, pinning up washing on a washing line in the pouring rain. This was an indicator perhaps, but not necessarily an authentic one. Whether the scene was true to life and, just as importantly, whether this really showed us anything of the character's inner world, is highly debatable.

We are not especially interested in making work that is 'about' learning disability. Nevertheless audiences do bring with them a set of assumptions, misperceptions and even stereotypes about learning disability. Since one of our aims is to facilitate and even authenticate the differing worldview and theatrical vision of the actor with a learning disability, the intention is not to have the audience oblivious to the fact that the actors do indeed have learning disabilities. On the other hand if this is all they see – or think they see – they will have learned (or seen) nothing beyond their own set of misapprehensions. They will, in fact, have failed to see the work and failed to see the actors as actors. Authenticity therefore takes on an extra importance for actors with learning disabilities. A poor or inauthentic performance by a well-known actor without a learning disability may be embarrassing or unsatisfying but there is little more at stake than the actor's own career. An inauthentic or 'poor' performance from an actor with a learning disability risks the actor, the entire cast and their work as a whole being dismissed as a charitable event or public spectacle better left to the drama therapy room – in effect barring actors with learning disabilities from professional status and leaving the audience completely unchanged.

Equally, it is certainly possible, with a great deal of effort and repetition and translation from the verbal to the physical, to elicit a plausible, conventional but wholly inauthentic performance from an actor with a learning disability. This risks reinforcing the perception of good theatre as rote-learning or 're-presentation' of a role, whilst effectively forcing actors with learning disabilities to produce theatre that is quite alien to them and is even misrepresentative of their worldview and perceptions – their 'ways of being' and 'ways of seeing'. In short, it is possible, with great effort, to encourage a relatively polished, conventional but ultimately empty performance that offers little to either actor or spectator, which may even reinforce the notion that professional theatre cannot be 'done' by actors with learning disabilities with any degree of profundity. The actor and audience remain unmoved.

In 2005, having worked with one of the author's companies in a series of script development sessions, the writer and actor Vanessa Rosenthal noted how:

> The company members I worked with brought a truthfulness and simplicity to their work. In response they demanded an openness, a truthfulness and a clarity that too often gets lost in 'tricks' by professionals. Nothing was a given: everything had to be earned through trust and mutual respect. I found the demands rigorous and humbling. In the days before I started the job I was somewhat sceptical of what I might gain personally ... but then I suddenly got it! The thing all actors chase as the elusive chimera is *communication* and in order to communicate one had to lose all sense of ego. They [the actors] gave utter, complete honesty and in order to meet that honesty one had to give the same back. No tricks. No mannerisms. Just *be*.[25]

Authenticity, as we have seen, is important to theatre generally. There may be even more at stake when it comes to actors with learning disabilities. Furthermore, by virtue of the nature of learning disability, overt re-presentation of clear-cut roles, disconnected to the actor, is completely at odds with the theatrical forms that come most readily to the actors. Having outlined the emergence of a theatre that overturns the old conventions to make way for new and more authentic performance forms, we want now to look more closely at the processes by which such work is enabled and devised. In the following chapters we therefore move directly into the studio, first locating the search for authenticity in practice.

4. Jon Tipton in Pinocchio, York Theatre Royal. © 2007 Karl Andre.

III

Understanding the Person, Preparing the Actor

When a group of actors meet for the first time in the rehearsal studio, they ordinarily bring with them a number of years of training and, often, experience. Yet because of the lack of access to formal training available to those with learning disabilities, it is inevitable that the director committed to working professionally with actors with learning disabilities will be starting from the very beginning. This situation reflects poorly on drama schools. Nevertheless it does also mean that the actors come without technical baggage and traditional notions of theatrical training. At this early stage of the process the director will be faced with the responsibility of choosing how to train the actors and asking which qualities they might want to develop. At the same time this provides the challenge and excitement of defining from the outset new and original training methods.

The participants, at this early stage, cannot strictly be called actors. They have expressed an interest in working as actors – surely a prerequisite to their presence in the studio – even if their notion of acting may be limited. Nor can we guarantee that all of the aspiring actors will, in the end, necessarily have the ability to practise professionally. The skills we advocate developing here are very different to those prized in conventional actor training methods and are governed by the attributes of the individual rather than the perceived demands of the profession. This does not mean, however, that professional notions of quality and commitment can be laid aside: to make concessions for poor work or lack of dedication from an actor with a learning disability is potentially to patronise that actor. It is also to let down those members of the group who really do demonstrate the necessary skill and commitment.

As such the director must be absolutely clear about his or her motivation for working with this particular group of actors. This is not drama as a social activity, nor is it therapy, even though many of the exercises will have a therapeutic value. It might be an exaggeration to call this early process an extended casting audition but, in a sense, it is. The director must do all that is possible to draw out the potential qualities, skills and attributes in each member of the group and must give the actors every opportunity to prove themselves before deciding whether or not they 'have what it takes'. Nevertheless by the end of this exploratory training period it may become clear that some of those involved are not going to develop into strong performers and in such cases a drama group or local amateur company might be a more appropriate outlet for their interest. If one wishes to achieve work of a high quality one must be prepared to set a level of skill and commitment against which the individual is measured. These may not be the *same* criteria as those used in more formal drama training but they should be equally robust.

We have discussed the problematic nature of equating access to theatre with access to *conventional* theatre, and highlighted the fact that conventional acting skills would provide an ill-fitting and inauthentic means of creative expression for those to whom these skills do not come naturally. As we have seen, many devised theatre ensembles have in any case chosen to move far beyond the traditional script-led model. When we talk of training people in the 'art' of acting, then, we are not talking about teaching skills such as articulation, learning lines, character motivation and so forth. We do not even advocate physical classes in any formal sense (for example, dance classes or Laban), although the body is central to the work in question. (If taught appropriately, with sensitivity and awareness of the overall aim of enabling free expression, then more formal classes can be useful at a later stage of training.) The director must be wary of arguing for a traditional approach to actor training in the name of equality of opportunity; we can only reiterate the fact there is nothing equal about access to what works for someone else but not for you. Furthermore attempts to shoehorn the actor with learning disabilities into conventional approaches might suggest a lack of vision on the part of the director, or a fear of going beyond what they themselves know, as well as an ingrained belief about the superior nature of conventional theatre.

We advocate an adapted model that arises from the needs and abilities of the individual performer on the grounds that an authentic performance will never come from imposing alien theatrical models on the actor. At the same time this adapted model, which is eminently suited to actors with learning disabilities, has proved to encourage particularly creative work from any actor prepared to enter into the process. The methods developed are not based on a rigid distinction between actors with learning disabilities and actors without and similarly non-traditional methods have been developed by a range of ensemble theatre companies. The methods we advocate are open and organic. By its very nature, then, this approach implies that there is no 'set' way of training the actor with a learning disability, or any actor for that matter. We would nevertheless suggest some basic principles that will be useful to any practitioner seeking to explore new approaches to making theatre.

Whilst moving away from conventional theatre training there are a number of 'qualities' that the director should look for and aim to draw out of the actors that equate favourably with traditional approaches. This is especially the case if they are seeking to train *creative* actors.[1] As with any trainee, time and commitment will be essential if the work is to develop. Those with original and perceptive ideas and, crucially, the ability to present these physically and with clarity to a spectator, will be better equipped to work as actors. At the same time actors must be able to do this without retreating into insularity; they will need to be willing to share with and adapt to others, to be emotionally generous, sympathetic and responsive. Theatre is after all a collaborative process. In the first instance this might simply be recognised as a willingness to be in the room with everyone else.

Alongside this are personal qualities such as a lack of ego, sensitivity and responsiveness, the ability to 'react' and respond genuinely rather than to 'act' and the ability (or at least potential) to enter into the process of releasing emotions and unblocking the barriers to full expression. These attributes are difficult to pin down and they may not be obvious or even present at the beginning of the process. It will take time to discover, for example, whether with support and encouragement a potential actor will be able to break down their defences and 'let go' of the 'blocks to authenticity'. Skills in expression and communication are crucial for any actor, yet these need not be verbal, and indeed are unlikely to be for many with learning disabilities. Verbal communication, in any case, frequently gets in the way of good theatre, a point we touched on in the last chapter and which we will explore in more depth in relation to physical communication. The requirements for communication and engagement with others might seem at first to bar out those with learning disabilities who appear to be insular and self-absorbed, traits that are traditionally ascribed to autism. We prefer to avoid such labels, however, and in our experience actors can be enabled to engage *regardless* of disability; it is simply that different techniques need to be employed for different people. We would suggest there are those without learning disabilities who are equally unable to communicate effectively with others, even with a full verbal range at their disposal. The ability or otherwise to communicate creatively is not tied rigidly into a disability but instead is an attribute of the individual.

All of these qualities are essential in preparing an actor for the processes of making theatre. Nevertheless, as we have suggested, such 'qualities' or abilities might not present themselves at first sight with actors with learning disabilities due to severe lack of self-esteem or confidence, which can also inhibit any awareness of external requirements. An actor might have interesting ideas and a desire to connect with others but at first be too shy to reveal themselves – this initial shyness can on occasion be extreme, with actors literally hiding from the group. Equally a person might have a strong desire to perform but at first be so self-conscious that they simply stand, motionless, while others look on. We have mentioned the importance of generosity: some people's generosity can border on unnecessary humility, so that they dismiss as worthless any thoughts of their own in favour of other people's. Likewise an actor with a strong desire to perform and a good awareness of public presentation might initially be unwilling or unable to reveal anything of their inner voice, and may even dominate the room by failing to respect that there are other people to consider. This can manifest itself in loud or 'manic' behaviour. Again, we must be careful not to tie such behaviours down to particular disabilities in a rigidly essentialist way, or to rely on labels. Aside from the problematic nature of subsuming people under the banner of specific diagnoses rather than approaching them as individuals, these labels can also encourage us to apprehend only what we *expect* to apprehend. We might then begin to dismiss any emerging quality that would seem not to fit with the person's 'diagnosis'. Insular actors can be – and have been – encouraged to share and open up, whilst loud and dominating actors usually (though not always) calm down once they are enabled to be more aware of others. This again highlights that the type of training we advocate is not comprised of a series of external tools but instead relies on encouraging awareness of self and others. As such many of the processes we describe will indeed be therapeutic, though this is not the end goal.

Such initial blocks or issues will be present in all novice performers: there will always be some whose initial idea of acting revolves around the notion of aggressively taking centre-stage and who will have to learn to engage with a group. Equally there will be those who wish to perform but for whom self-consciousness is at first a barrier. Anybody working in community theatre will have come across such problems. However they can be more obviously manifest, and more extreme, with actors with learning disabilities. On the one hand it is at least clear to the director which qualities will need to be developed; on the other hand, the training period can be particularly challenging and lengthy and requires genuine dedication on the part of both actor and director. We would argue that actors with learning disabilities have every right to a long and committed training period. Those with access to conventional acting training will commit to at least three years of study. We see no reason to scrimp therefore with training when it comes to actors with learning disabilities, even if this training may be of a radically different nature.

The focus for the work described in this chapter is primarily on the development of the individual within the context of the group. The chapters that follow will go on to discuss the development into true ensemble group work. This shift from individual to group, and from private concerns to wider interests and issues, also parallels that of the development of a company from its early beginnings. Even when showing professional work, a 'young' ensemble might find that the first few shows are primarily explorations of the individuals before they become ready to tell stories and describe scenarios that lie beyond their own personal experience. This does not mean that these early shows cannot be professional theatre but simply that in the development of the individual actors, as well as the group as a whole, a turning point will eventually be reached at which the work takes on a wider remit. This also parallels the development of those political theatres we have already discussed whose early, agenda-driven work, despite being concerned with the world, nevertheless took its impetus from the particular political issues that directly affected its members. Many of these groups later began to make work that engaged in more complex ways with wider political, aesthetic and theatrical themes.

At this early stage, however, the director will be largely concerned with discovering, nurturing and releasing those qualities and attributes we have talked about and with allowing the actor free reign to explore very personal issues and experiences. In a sense this early training is simply about getting to know the actors, as well as encouraging the actors to get to know each other and promoting increased awareness of the group dynamic. These are achieved through building rapport and trust, removing blocks to authenticity, freeing up the actors, and exploring physicality and vocals, as well as certain useful warm-up techniques. The emphasis will be on non-verbal communication and on beginning to shape a shared theatrical vision. The first port of call for any actor wishing to work creatively will always, however, be themselves; in order to make good work as an actor it will be essential, first and foremost, to begin to break down the blocks and barriers to true creative and emotional expression.

Expression and Release

As we have established, authenticity is for us the key to strong performance; effective communication, too, is essential: it is no good, after all, being authentic on your own. We have talked about the barriers to authenticity that are present to one degree or another in all of us: socialisation, poor self-esteem, self-consciousness, anxiety, an inability to 'let go' and to be in the moment, and so on. The director's job is to eradicate these blocks as far as possible, and this will be the same for any director seeking authentic performances from any actor or group of actors. As we discussed in the last chapter, actors with learning disabilities may find this process both more and less difficult than non-disabled actors. On the one hand, having not reached the same level of self-conscious socialisation and 'accomplishment' as others, barriers such as an over-reliance on verbal eloquence will not be present to the same degree. On the other hand the release of unexpressed emotions and the expression of previously buried aspects of the self have the potential to be disturbing, and especially so for someone who may have bottled up years of difficult emotions. Without full access to verbal expression and knowing of no other socially 'accepted' communication style, the actors will have had no adequate outlet through which to release buried emotions and sensations or through which to express their imagination. The process therefore requires great sensitivity and responsiveness, trust and rapport, and the importance of the director's receptivity and integrity in relation to the actors' expression cannot be overestimated. Rapport can mean simply allowing things to be 'okay', validating and responding (without, instead, judging what an appropriate response might be or look like) and following the lead of the individual.

Because of this the emotional environment is crucial. It is the director's role to establish a welcoming, encouraging, supportive and enjoyable atmosphere. Fun is important partly because the work can be emotionally difficult. It is also important because, in these early stages, we are simply trying to get to know one another: this can even involve basic non-theatrical activities such as eating together, taking journeys together, dancing, even just 'hanging out' – allowing ourselves just to 'be'. Such activities in the first instance take the pressure off the actors, who may otherwise feel that they are required to 'do' or 'produce' or 'perform', and allow them to gain social confidence (especially where this may be lacking). They also allow the actors to begin to take ownership of the rehearsal space and the processes that take place within it.

Likewise the director's attitudes, manner and demeanour – the 'energy' he or she is bringing into the room – have a distinct effect on those of other people. The director needs to lead the group without dominating it, to be willing to make mistakes and not to take him or herself too seriously. He or she must also ensure that each individual is valued and be careful not to use words which might disempower an actor. In general the director will strive to be present in the room on the same level as the actors whilst, in a significant sense, searching for the most appropriate way of communicating with each individual. He or she will seek to work *alongside* the actors, being willing to copy and to be copied, and to avoid imposing or encouraging overt hierarchies, instead aiming to dispel any 'mystique' surrounding the notion of theatre. (If we truly believe in Peter Brook's observation that theatre is created the moment someone is observed crossing a stage, then there should be nothing mysterious about it.) The director should not expect an actor to do anything he or she would not do themselves and this is best achieved by showing solidarity with the group through joining in the activities. This is also the only way in which the director can get into the 'head state' of the actor and begin to empathise with the actor's unique issues, experiences and perceptions.

If we suspend judgment at this early stage we are able not only to validate the actor's subjective experience but also to truly get to know the actor, to find out more about who he or she really is and what his or her individual strengths and potential might be. All too often a director will set up a seemingly open-ended scenario and then proceed to make judgments about responses that fall outside the range of those expected. If, say, a director asks an actor to copy or mirror a movement, or to engage with something, or to make eye contact, but that actor instead does absolutely nothing, refusing to engage with the task or instead looking away, many directors would perceive this lack of response as a 'failure'. Yet for us during this process *any* contribution should be accepted and explored, even if this may be a 'negative' offering or engagement. This lack of response (or invisible response, since we cannot know just by watching what someone is actually feeling or thinking) is valid – and validated – precisely *as* a response, as an act of communication, at least during this formative period. (If after many months of training a person is still unable or unwilling to respond, we might then of course have to reconsider the possibility of their working as an actor.) Negative communication at this early stage may even prove a starting-point for the development of a (perhaps entirely non-verbal) dialogue, and effective communication between actor and director at this point is the foundation of the work. Since our aim is to allow the actor full expression, to encourage their access to authentic emotional release, it is also the director's role to assist the actor in going further. As well as *allowing* and validating any contribution (we are not talking here about *verbally* praising the actor) the director might also suggest extending that contribution further.

Complex games and exercises, as well as the introduction of props, objects and costumes, can be unhelpful at this stage. Whilst it may be tempting to want to 'get to work' on making theatre in this way, to do so is both to misunderstand the raw material of theatre and to miss out a crucial stage in the journey. Whilst these elements can be useful as the work develops and the actors gain confidence and trust, in this formative period the group requires instead the minimum of distraction and pressure. When the actors have not yet fully developed their imaginative potential, props and costume can even have a deadening rather than liberating effect, putting blocks on the scope of the imagination; they can also serve to conceal a lack of genuine exploration of authenticity on the part of the director. A deckchair and an umbrella, for example, will almost inevitably suggest a stereotypical improvisation about 'a day at the seaside' and our aim at this stage is to discover what is unusual and atypical about the individual, not to show that they are able to produce a pastiche of seaside manners. Even where props are later introduced it is important that they are used as external focal points for expression or in order to draw out expressive potential rather than as limiting impositions. We shall return to the importance of the choice of props, music and other starting points in the following chapter.

Instead we would advocate working primarily from the physical. The raw materials for theatre-making are in any case already there in the room in the form of the actors themselves: their physicalities and personalities and the experiences and histories that they bring into the studio. Indeed the focus for the work at this stage should remain on the development of dialogue – whether this be physical or, occasionally, verbal – regardless of whatever else may be present in the room. The aim is to begin to 'prepare' the actor for theatre-making through the use of the senses – sounds, facial expression, touch, emotion – and to do this we must also begin to break down those barriers we have discussed: shyness, self-consciousness, social restraints and restrictions. Despite our emphasis on bodily, sensory and visual approaches, for those actors with a certain measure of verbal ability, personal stories can be one way of validating the individual whilst also getting to know them better. These need not be complex; in simply asking an actor to show the group what they have inside their pocket or handbag an entire narrative may emerge. The simplest items can contain deeply personal meanings. A front door key might contain within it a story about independence and respect, whilst a lunch box might reveal the owner's feelings about living with the fact that people think they are overweight. This exercise, through peer example, might also encourage those with less verbal skill to share their own particular object because whilst they may not be able to verbalise their response they nevertheless understand the point of the exercise. The director in turn can then help to validate this response in other ways. These sorts of exercises can be fruitful starting points for making theatre. More importantly, however, they are simple means by which to allow people to reveal themselves.

Getting to know the actors as individuals is important for another reason, especially where a director may not have worked with actors with learning disabilities before. Particularly with people with more severe or visible learning disabilities, the director, despite their own good intentions, may find themselves struggling to see beyond the disability and its particular effects. (Nevertheless we are not suggesting that the disability is not also a part of who the actor is and of their experience of the world.) This veneer must be broken through and true rapport gained, and this rapport will be as important for the director as it is for the actor. Furthermore when an actor does begin to release previously unexpressed material or emotions – anger, perhaps, or sadness – the director must be able to empathise with the actor, simply to be there without judgment. He or she must at the same time overcome any impulse to halt a session for fear it is becoming 'too intense' or stepping too far outside the boundaries of the theatrical encounter. Without some real engagement with our emotional life we cannot create authentic theatre. At the same time we must, as actors, be able to recreate a full range of emotion onstage; in other words we have to learn to manage our emotions effectively. Since people with learning disabilities have often been denied access to their own emotions, they also tend to have little experience of managing or containing them. As directors in this context we will be required to tackle this issue head-on.

This may all sound highly 'therapeutic'; if it is, then it is therapy at the service of theatre, with emotions being expressed rather than 'analysed' or 'dealt with'. As such the work can at first be difficult for those who are new to it. For these reasons the preparation of the director should also be borne in mind. Crucially, the director must be willing to suspend their own notions of 'correct' responses and to begin to engage empathically with the actors. Ultimately it is about seeing the relationship between director and actor as an equal interaction between two human beings with a shared desire to explore how they might best communicate with one another.

Preparing the Director? Understanding Empathy

Due to the very particular demands of this approach to actor training, the director will find that a hands-off, cool, distant or overly objective stance becomes not only undesirable but impossible. Nor is this work for the un-inquisitive or faint-hearted. The director will not be immune from the process of self-discovery; in engaging with others and their very different inhabitation of the world the director will also ideally come to experience and understand themselves more fully. It is important, too, to remember that although the focus is on the individual at this stage, the process always happens in the context of the group, of which the director is also a member. Much of what each individual discovers and learns about him or herself and about how to communicate is significantly enhanced by group working; indeed empathy is meaningless without engagement with others.

Empathy is crucial yet it is also a difficult concept. We may feel we are *empathising* when in fact we are *sympathising*, trying to understand another's experience through direct comparisons with our own. Such an approach frequently results in profound misunderstandings and a measure of judgment, since it always inevitably means that we fail to respect the other person's radically different nature and experiences. Empathy is instead about allowing that another may have a different outlook to one's own, respecting its validity, and attempting, also, to put oneself in somebody else's very different shoes. *You* might express rage through shouting; *I* might express rage through silence. On the contrary, silence for me might express contentment; another might assume that contentment should always be verbalised and take another's silence as an expression of disapproval or boredom. Yet silence will not mean the same thing to two different people and to assume so can result in a comedy of errors, at the least, or more damaging consequences at worst. True engagement with another can therefore never be approached without a measure of empathy. It is also untrue, in our experience, to suggest that certain learning disabilities by definition hamper the ability to be empathic. Even the most insular individual can learn a measure of empathy and the fact that we cannot see this may instead reflect our own lack of empathy in looking for it in all the wrong places.

Especially where our primary means of communication has been verbal, it may be difficult to understand how to empathise with someone who is not speaking, or to imagine that they, in turn, may be able to empathise with us. But the possibility of communication contains the seeds of empathy within it, so that empathy might be expressed physically as much as verbally. Where the director wishes to see an actor flesh out or go further with what he or she is expressing, the director must do this intuitively, without imposition and preferably through gesture or other non-verbal means. The director might then attempt to embody this expression himself, working in conjunction with the actor. Mirroring can be one of the most important and useful exercises for building empathy as well as trust and rapport. The game 'Walk My Walk', discussed later, is just one example of how to do this.

Likewise if at this early stage an actor is unable to join in with the work, or seems to be immune to attempts on the director's part to empathise or connect, it may simply be that the director is trying to empathise on his or her own terms. This is by definition a contradiction. If an actor sits in silence in a corner, and the director simply joins them, a form of empathy has already been exchanged via simple bodily means. In any case, because of their conceptual nature and the way in which they can delineate or close down meaning, words are often the least effective means of empathising with others – for this reason amongst others we advocate a primarily non-verbal approach.

Full Body Expression: A Non-Verbal Approach

People with learning disabilities have often had difficulties finding an appropriate means of communication, particularly if their verbal skills are limited. They may have difficulties storing information; recalling words from a 'memory bank'; sequencing words to construct anything other than the simplest of sentences; or they may have a related physical impairment that hinders the physical act of forming sounds and words. In addition the social stigma of these difficulties often contributes to a profound lack of confidence from an early age, further inhibiting the capacity to learn. To note these facts, is, however, far from suggesting that people with learning disabilities *cannot* communicate. Many with learning disabilities find coherent speaking difficult; on the other hand there are those with learning disabilities who are vocal in the extreme. In either case to communicate without (we prefer 'beyond') words has significant advantages. For those with severe difficulties with speech, working non-verbally not only removes any pressure to speak effectively but provides other means of expression that the person may never have been previously 'offered' as valid modes of communication. For these actors bodily expression allows a form of authentic communication that comes more easily than words and the discovery of other means of effective expression can have profound effects, allowing the release of emotions that have been suppressed for some time. This access to expression is therefore also a validation of them as human beings. On the other hand for those inclined to extreme verbosity, working beyond words can allow the release of inner emotions that are perhaps disguised by an *excessive* use of language.

A non-verbal approach has proven useful and creative for actors with learning disabilities, and has grown from a response to the actors' needs. Yet such an approach can be profoundly liberating for any actor, especially those who have donned the guises of other characters and their attendant soliloquies in order to escape from rather than to explore their own personality. Words can be an inadequate representation of what is really happening between people – body language, as we know, reveals truths that words may conceal craftily (just as Freudian slips reveal that what we are saying is not always, if ever, exactly what we are thinking). Words can lie to us – hence we try to 'read between the lines'. For some of us words may come easily but may not mean much; for others words can be a frustration and are simply inadequate as a primary means of communication. Furthermore we can often subtly govern other people's behaviour through the words we use to describe it. In response those people begin to behave in ways that reinforce our mistaken perceptions. This is particularly true when we label people in any way – and nowhere truer, perhaps, than the ways in which we have traditionally labelled people with learning disabilities.

Working 'beyond words' is not a mere necessity but, for us, an active and positive approach to theatre-making. We believe that there is a significant range of experience that not only does not require words in order to be expressed but which may be more *fully* expressed through other means, and we are interested in making theatre that reflects this. Our society holds a prejudice whereby if we see two people together and one is using words and the other is not, it is assumed that the one who speaks is the more intelligent. Yet it is as likely that someone who cannot express themselves well verbally will have the potential to communicate the full range of experience more effectively, and by more varied means, than someone who is limited by their skills in verbal articulation.

For actors without learning disabilities this way of working will probably run contrary to conventional training. They will also have become reliant on words as the dominant form of communication, so that the process is complicated by the need to undo some of their training and current practice (as well as to work against the dominant form of communication in everyday life). Working with the body as the primary tool for communication is liberating in that it allows for work that is more open to interpretation whilst at the same time being more challenging. If in a workshop setting, for example, and the director gives no verbal instructions, it becomes the actor's responsibility to create something; this can be difficult, even exposing, for actors used to being told what to do by a director. To not know what is wanted of you may be akin to travelling without a map; indeed, our personalities are formed in response to the perceived demands of parents and society and to have no guidance in childhood can be damaging. As adults, however, it is essential if we are to truly know ourselves (and therefore to be truly creative) and to cast off the 'mirrors' held up by those around us. We need to learn to act (in both senses of the word) on our own intuition and without the comforting, yet also controlling, guidance and expectations of others. Insisting that the actor steps outside his or her comfort zone is ultimately rewarding, just as the traveller who leaves their map and guide book at home will encounter new and unexplored territory.

In order to get to know ourselves effectively – which, for us, is key to 'creative' theatre-making – it is essential then to trust one's own instincts. At the same time, however, total insularity and disregard for others can be damaging and equally constraining. We have also to learn how to communicate effectively with other people: how can we know what we feel if we do not express it? (We may be quietly confident that we are courageous enough to make a difficult request, for example, but it is only in the act of doing so that we truly reveal our courage or lack of it.) In communicating with others we discover that our own deeply held views or opinions are not the only ones; we may even find that they are not even authentically ours. By definition, differing viewpoints make apparent the constructed nature of our beliefs and personalities and the fact that we are not 'fully formed' but always in the process of becoming. In turn this allows us to explore how we come to be who we are and to tap into our individual potential.

Whilst talking is one way of getting to know each other, it is not necessarily the most effective or revealing means of communication. We can be easily duped by words – particularly if we only attend to their literal meaning and not to the person and their attendant body language. As Jacques Lecoq states: 'the body knows things about which the mind is ignorant'.[2] Working within physical theatre we begin to develop a sense for the truth of physical movement – and to discover that it is almost impossible to lie with our bodies. We can spot immediately if a person is not truthful in the movement he or she is making. The body is always in more direct and immediate contact with the impulse that produces a response than is verbal language, through which we can consciously or unconsciously disguise what we really feel. This is why the revelations of body language experts can be both shocking and embarrassing – we perhaps do not realise how much we give away with our bodily movements and how easily we belie our ulterior motives. We are generally taught not to trust this sense, yet it is the job of the director to function on this intuitive level in the search for authenticity. The body has its own language and one that must be communicated with on its own terms.

The relationship between the mind and the body is complex, and to do justice to the various arguments surrounding that relationship would be impossible in this context. The conventional separation of the two (the 'Cartesian' dichotomy of which we have spoken) has been overturned in the twentieth century by numerous thinkers and bodies of thought, not least the phenomenology of those such as Merleau-Ponty, for whom 'all the creativity and free-ranging mobility that we have come to associate with the human intellect is, in truth, an elaboration, or recapitulation, of a profound creativity already underway at the most immediate level of sensory perception'.[3] Psychoanalytic thought, however flawed, has also posited a profound connection between the body and the mind. Psychoanalysis inevitably argues for a release of trapped bodily impulses through words, 'the talking cure', and even goes so far as to suggest that the unconscious itself is 'structured as a language' (e.g. in the work of analyst and thinker Jacques Lacan). Psychoanalytic models are useful for many; for those who have difficulty speaking, however, such models will be less than fruitful.

As against conventional talking therapies, drama therapy, psychodrama and the 'dreambody' work of Arnold Mindell and Marie-Louise von Franz all employ bodily expression to release emotions. By contrast to traditional Freudian, Jungian or even Lacanian thought, whereby trapped bodily impulses are released through speaking, for the likes of Mindell effective therapy is instead achieved by encouraging the 'patient' to explore their situation physically, theatrically and, crucially, *without words*. Such therapies will be better suited to those for whom verbal expression is difficult if not impossible; we have also found that emotional release can be effected through the body alone, especially where that body begins to utilise its own language. As we have stated, the methods proposed in this book are not primarily intended to serve a therapeutic end, however we would argue that a certain element of release is a prerequisite for becoming an actor. The non-verbal, non-instructive approach also has the advantage of allowing the work to move organically from one stage into the next. The use of words and verbal instructions, by contrast, can disrupt or even abruptly destroy the momentum and energy of the process.

Dymphna Callery has described the motivation of much of the work of physical theatre companies as being the desire to find a different and perhaps more meaningful kind of truth through physical exploration. Here theatre becomes:

a commitment to the concept of the creative actor, to a physical approach to performance where language is only one of the performance elements, to the notion that within every actor lies creative potential which can be accessed through imaginative play.[4]

We are similarly interested in redressing the balance between the body and mind, in reconnecting the two and even reasserting the primacy of the body. Of course it would be virtually impossible for most of us to conduct every aspect of our lives without words, and the processes here are no exception. Tasks are set, instructions occasionally given, but these are the tip of the iceberg in terms of what the truth of the interactions in the room are really about. Ideally a verbal instruction will only be used to clarify the openness of an exercise, that is, to re-enforce the fact that one is inviting a creative response rather than determining what the outcome might be. The degree to which words are necessary in both the rehearsal room and the performance will be discovered, like all other aspects, through the process. It is not a rule or a given but a challenge, a process of discovery. For the director it can be a revelation to attempt to run a session with as few words as possible.

This non-verbal approach extends, for us, throughout the entire devising process. In this sense the work we advocate in this book has much in common with that of other physical theatre practitioners. What is perhaps unique to our approach is that words are not only *not* the dominant form of communication between characters and in the action, they are also *not* the dominant form of communication between the actors and the director in the rehearsal room. Working with actors with learning disabilities, work will not be 'analysed' verbally but instead through repetition. Returning to a particular scene the work may begin to move in a different direction – any analysis or reflection will, however, have been intuitive rather than conceptual. In such work words cannot be relied on to effectively set up an exercise, to talk through character, plot or relationship, to develop narrative or to fine-tune a scene. It is incumbent on the director to trust the intuitive process and to utilise his or her skills to facilitate this non-verbal approach to revisiting and revising material, rather than imposing concepts or overviews on the developing work. This is not the only way of working, of course, and ultimately it may not be an approach that all practitioners wish to take. We , however, have found that it produces highly creative work.

The commitment to finding ways of communicating without words extends out of the devising process and becomes part of the everyday interaction within the rehearsal room. Nevertheless in the studio at this early stage it is enough that verbal dialogue is replaced by physical dialogue as the primary means of communication. One of the simplest ways we have found to develop physical work is through the use of mirroring, which, as we have suggested, is also central to a non-verbal approach to encouraging empathy and rapport.

Mirroring and Copying

Books on 'how to win friends and influence people' have long advocated mirroring techniques in order to build rapport. This can be a cynical and manufactured way of promoting empathy, nevertheless it is based on a fundamental truth that mirroring and mimicry allow us to connect with the 'mindset' and embodied subjectivity of another person. Mirroring is one aspect of the broader notion of 'copying', a significant technique at the director's disposal for developing communication, particularly in these early stages. In simple mirroring exercises (which can make very effective warm-up techniques), the person being mirrored becomes aware of the fact that their movements, however tiny and involuntary, are perceptible and therefore significant. For the person doing the mirroring, the exercise reveals the way in which other people move differently, have different 'energies' and impulses and differently inhabit the world. By trying to mirror someone else we are, in effect, empathising with that person through understanding what it is like to be in their body; we are also communicating with them on the simplest yet most fundamental of levels. In the act of mirroring we begin to discover these similarities and differences and to reflect on ourselves. Mimicry is a more playful and mischievous version of mirroring. It involves a degree of exaggeration that, if done with sensitivity, can further break down tension and blocks.

Copying and mirroring have other advantages. Just as meditation can switch off the rational mind and alleviate anxiety, so too can copying. For the copier there is no requirement to think other than to concentrate on copying as precisely as possible. For the 'copied' there is the possibility of being naturally alerted to unconscious and habituated ways of moving. The unconscious set of bodily movements or mannerisms that we daily carry with us has been termed the 'dreambody' by Arnold Mindell and Marie-Louise von Franz.[5] The 'dreambody' is not dissimilar to the body as discussed by Freud, which holds psychic impulses within itself and which therefore embodies our psychical state. Nevertheless, for Mindell this dreambody can be negotiated, communicated with and released *on its own terms* rather than via the extra stratum of language. Chris Johnston has highlighted the way in which, in allowing our bodies to be animated by somebody else's movements, we are able to relinquish control of our own movements:

> When we copy, we give ourselves over to being directed so the body relaxes. It gets time off from constantly supervising its action regime. We're released from decisions about how to move and what to say … in the emptiness created movements which are not consciously organised may be allowed to emerge.[6]

Copying can be as simple as sitting in pairs opposite each other and mirroring the gestures of another. A more overt copying exercise is 'Walk My Walk', discussed by Johnston, in which one person walks as naturally as possible whilst another person follows and attempts to copy them. Although this is perhaps better tried once a certain amount of confidence and trust has been built, since it can be regarded as threatening, exposing or even as mockery if rapport has not already been established, the exercise reveals our unique ways of walking. 'Walk My Walk' can be great fun, of course, since copying someone always has the potential for humour, though we would advocate against mimicry unless or until the group is secure in their respect for one another and the purpose of the work. Yet there is much more than relaxed fun going on here. The person being copied has the revealing experience of seeing 'themselves' walking around the room. They become aware of how they appear or present

5. *Development workshop with* Pinocchio *actors at York Theatre Royal.*
© 2006 Joan Russell.

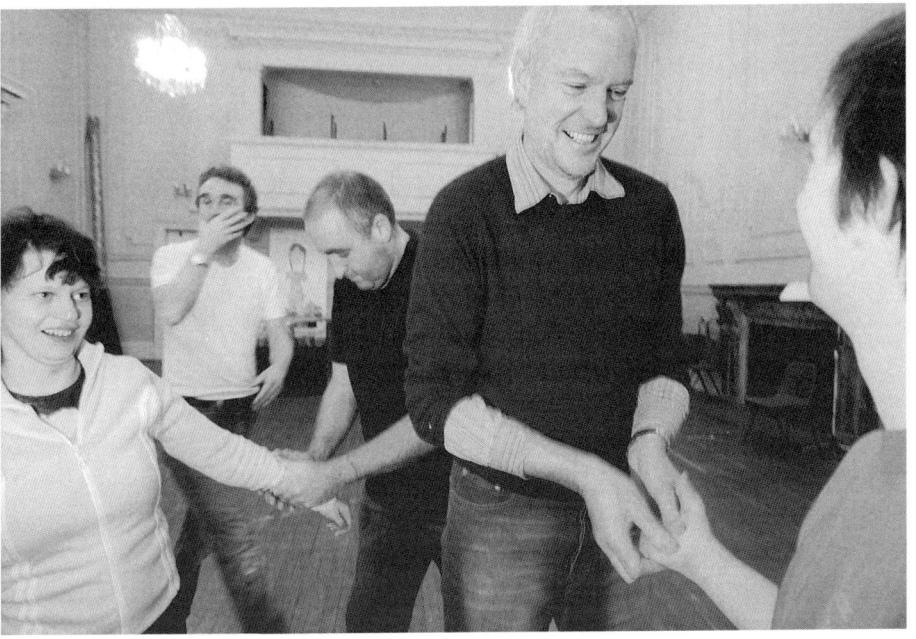

6. *Stage Exchange Workshop, York Theatre Royal.* © 2005 Joan Russell.

themselves to others and through this de-naturalisation become aware of aspects of themselves that have been taken for granted ('do I *really* slouch/ hobble/ teeter/ bounce?'). The person doing the copying is able, if only briefly, to inhabit the physical world of another, at the same time letting go of their own deeply ingrained physical style. For both copier and copied, the particularities of physicality are overtly revealed. From simple mirroring it is also possible to extend an exercise to moving in complimentary ways: if one person stretches up the other might crouch down; if one bends one way the other might bend in the opposite direction. In this way it is also quite easy to create the beginnings of authentic dance.

If our mannerisms and bodily habits reveal our inner emotions and daily experience of living, it follows that we can also change our emotions through a change in bodily manner. If we fake a behaviour, we can be surprised how easily it becomes real. If we force ourselves to smile, we are often surprised to find that we start to feel a little happier. If we purposely stoop and sulk and pout, we are likely to start to feel depressed. We begin to *feel* differently; in a small way, too, we discover how it feels, quite literally, to be somebody else. Extending such an exercise to inventing or fabricating a completely new way of walking or moving, the imagination also begins to come into play. We become aware of our potential to create. In this simple exercise we encounter new ways of communicating and expressing ourselves, transcending our habitual, and habituated, ways of being. If we can learn to move differently, we can also learn to *be* differently.

The 'Walk My Walk' exercise is also about more than movement and empathy. In exercises like this we find the seeds of characterisation, since if our bodily styles and movements are intimately connected to our 'person' then a fabricated bodily style will begin to create a character. This is not about physical ability or stylish movement; we might pretend to limp, for example, and begin to understand what having a limp might feel like, albeit that such an experience will be temporary. This idea of characterisation need not even be bodily and could also be extended into the vocal realm without still falling back on verbal meaning: speaking the same words in a very different way, whilst using a particular dialect or 'lingo' also helps to build characterisation.

As Guy Dartnell notes, 'if you repeat a sound or a movement over and over again, you start to learn what the emotion of that sound is.'[7]

Another simpler version of a structured copying exercise is what has become known as 'The Warm-Up'.[8] Although less specific than 'Walk My Walk' it is in fact more exposing in that it encourages total free expression on the part of the person being copied. The group form a circle and one person is invited to come into the middle. They have permission to do anything they choose, be it: a physical exercise; a series of actions; making vocal sounds; creating rhythms with the body or beating on the floor. (The possibilities are only limited by the imagination and creativity of the individuals involved). The only 'rule' is that everyone has to copy precisely the actions of the person in the middle and must not try and influence what happens. When the person tires of being in the middle, or the facilitator senses that the group is losing focus, then the individual changes places with someone else in the group, choosing who they would like to go next. The exercise continues until everyone in the group has had a turn. Once the format has been established it is possible to run the entire exercise without any verbal instructions.

In the early stages of working with a group a lot of encouragement may be required, as a common response from the person in the middle is: 'I don't know what to do'. Sometimes, with a particularly shy individual for example, it may be enough for them simply to remain motionless and silent. But even this is valid if everyone in the group also remains motionless and silent for the time that the individual is in the middle. The essential point is that for that moment they are the focus of attention and they determine what happens in the space. At a more sophisticated level the exercise can develop individual awareness of the whole group (where people can challenge others to go beyond their 'comfort zone' or develop core performance skills such as extreme physicality or voice projection and articulation). It can also help to develop awareness of structure and form (in the choice of who is an appropriate person to be next in the middle to change the dynamic or develop an emerging theme).

It is important to remember that copying exercises are not about accurate mirroring. In the early stages it is also important that the focus remains on 'doing' rather than on 'remembering what to do'. Johnston refers to the 'emotional spirit' or 'quality of feeling' of the movement and this is what the actor is after, rather than an impressive display of perfect mechanical mimicry.[9] It is also this 'emotional spirit' or energy that contains the seeds of either empathy or character. Copying contains both question and answers and in this sense becomes a form of conversation or relationship. It also allows the actors to begin to develop ideas, imagination and characterisation whilst having their early contributions validated.

Provocations and Interventions

Even when using words, or word-based exercises, we would advocate using them to break down rather than shore up the logic of language. Nonsense games such as 'This Is My Nose', in which the actor points to a body part that is precisely *not* their nose whilst making the statement can be humorous provocations that highlight the absurdity of language when it is 'incorrectly' used. On the other hand, games that ordinarily use language and may be familiar to practitioners in devised or physical theatre can be reworked such that they draw the focus back to the body. The image games discussed at length by Johnston, presumably familiar to most students and practitioners, can just as easily be employed without the use of language. Instead of 'freeze-framing' a living tableau and giving it a verbal description, another actor might instead take up the position of one of the members of the 'scene' and then proceed to move it in a different direction. Here language is avoided altogether and any interpretation that the physical scenario provokes will be felt intuitively and, importantly, through the body. This game also has the advantage of further validating the individual's contribution and encouraging their ability to trust their instincts and ideas without necessarily having to 'explain' them.

We have said that this early work is better facilitated without the use of props and other interventions. Nevertheless if introduced in the right way they can be used as simple provocations in order to encourage release, expression, imagination and physicality. It is far better that the object is introduced as a thing in itself, to be explored for its potential, resonance and physicality, than as a necessary piece of equipment for a scene. So, for example, a chair might be brought into an improvisation not because someone needs to sit down in the work but so that the group can explore it beyond its functionality. A simple chair can transform itself in our collective imagination, thereby allowing us to develop work in other creative directions. A chair can be sat on but it can also be stood on, stood behind, crawled under, jumped over, and turned upside down or on its side. A chair can become a boat, a cage, a drum and so on. Objects and music can be starting points for making theatre, as we describe in depth later; at this stage, however, they have a different purpose and the choice of objects and music will therefore also be different.

Fun, upbeat, even 'silly' music – jingles from advertisements, for example – can be useful in encouraging people to let go and enjoy themselves, as can clapping and making random noises, whilst disco music immediately invites the notion of 'dancing'. This sort of music is unlikely to begin to create interesting theatre or to encourage any form of emotional narrative to emerge but it can be useful for releasing energy. The aim here is again to discourage thought or reflection and instead to allow the actors to focus on experiencing and to respond to the moment. It is important to keep the primary focus on 'doing' rather than thinking.

The newspaper game is another interesting example of a provocation. Here a newspaper is manipulated to become any number of things – a hat, an umbrella, a telescope, a blanket and so on. Far from being an origami exercise, the manipulation of the paper again allows us to move the focus away from thinking and into *doing*; the director should be careful not to allow the process to become too precious or thoughtful. Even if an actor only ends up copying what someone else has already done, it can nevertheless mean they have been able to engage with what the other person has imagined. Copying someone else's imagination may be the most authentic response for that person at this early stage, and that in itself should be validated. For another person, however, this response may be an inauthentic 'cop-out'. It is up to the director to intuit the difference and, in the latter case, to find an appropriate way of moving the individual towards greater authenticity. In this game the imagination is brought into play, and there is no reason why this might not then lead into a starting point for making theatre, even though this is not the primary aim. The processes we describe are organic and the divisions between stages are not so clear-cut in practice.

There are a wide range of games and exercises the director can choose to introduce at this early, experimental stage; such games are easy to come by and we list a number of useful sources at the end of this book. Phelim McDermott, Guy Dartnell and others have all discussed games and exercises whose primary aim is to free up the actors and to take the onus away from 'coming up with something'. Nevertheless it is crucial that the director chooses appropriately and also that they take as far as possible an organic approach. There is little point in playing such games for their own sake, especially if the level of sophistication or confidence required in order to make them effective is inappropriate to the stage the actors have reached, or if they require too much thought on the part of the actor. This is precisely the conscious reflection that they are designed to avoid. Complex ideas need to be developed gradually and the ways in which such games are played are just as important as the games themselves.

Many games have been developed that rely on assumptions that we already understand how to play them. For example, commonly used games such as those involving swapping chairs (e.g. 'Fruitbowl' or 'The Sun Shines On…') assume that everyone knows how to 'swap chairs' in the first place. If this is not the case, it is far better to improvise a game based on this idea, in order to develop an understanding of it, than to try to explain the rules. In the act of improvising such a game, new discoveries can be made about people, communication and interaction. Often games are difficult to play because they involve too many concepts and preconceived notions to allow easy assimilation. The act of dissecting them can be a creative act rather than a process of 'dumbing-down'.

Likewise it would be fruitless to stop a game simply because it had begun to develop in a different direction. The aim is not to impose exercises on the actors in order to extract specific outcomes.

Instead the appropriateness or usefulness of a particular exercise should always be led by the needs of the individuals and if an exercise naturally turns into some other kind of activity then perhaps that is the direction the group instinctively want it take. The director's role is to remain aware of what is 'going on' for the actors in a particular encounter or experience – true of games as of any other interaction. It is not the director's role to necessarily dictate the course of the work so much as to ensure that the direction it takes is interesting. If the activity loses direction completely, if the purpose is completely lost, then it can still be a fruitful experience: the individual actors then have to learn to take responsibility for giving the activity a fresh focus. Very little verbalisation should be necessary, since the director will always be reacting to the situation, intuitively sensing where the session might go next. Whilst it is useful for the director to have an armoury of games at his or her disposal, it is important to remember that these can be played in different ways and for different reasons at different stages of the process, or can be adapted, developed and invented as required. This early work is always, fundamentally, *about* the actors. Games and other exercises should never be allowed to dominate; they should instead remain at the service of the actors' needs.

This early work requires a great deal of trust on the part of both actor and director, with trust extending, too, to the director's belief in his or her own skills and instincts. Theatre-making is to a large extent an intuitive process and we reiterate throughout this book the importance of keeping this process as fluid as possible. Nevertheless by this stage the actors will have reached a certain level of sophistication – not in 'how to make theatre' but in terms of how to 'be themselves'. They will have grown in confidence and come to understand the dynamics of the group; they will also have begun to work with their imaginations. 'Tuned in' to the group dynamic and 'warmed up' for creative work, the ensemble is now ready to turn their focus toward creating theatre for an audience. In order to do this, a starting point is required.

7. Director Jon Palmer in rehersals with actors from *Full Body and the Voice*. © 2004 Patrick Fabre.

IV
Starting Points

Having arrived at the stage where the members of the group are familiar with one another, and comfortable with a particular way of communicating, we need to have an external focus for the work; to begin to look beyond the self to communicate meaningfully and purposefully with others – ultimately, our audiences. The transition from getting to know one another and warming up to beginning to make work is also echoed in the general trajectory of a company. With a developing ensemble, the first shows will necessarily in part be an exploration of who the individuals are and also a time during which the actors begin to find their artistic voices. There are three levels that the novice actor will attain: exploring first the individual and then the dynamics of the group, and finally beginning to explore wider issues and themes beyond the personal. They will only progress from one to the other when they are comfortable and ready. This will be the case for all ensemble theatre groups but it is perhaps more marked for a company of actors with learning disabilities; in addition, for a company whose members are initially untrained in theatre, the third level may even be said to mark the point at which the actor moves beyond being a community arts client to being a professional. Other factors are of course relevant here, including production standards and the payment of the actors, and these will be discussed fully in our final chapter. The point is that beyond the initial stages of familiarisation with each other and their own working methods, the group will begin to move towards making theatre for a paying public.

By this stage, also, the actors will have come to understand the director's own preferred 'language'. A director will always have his or her own preferences in terms of working methods and, again, this is little different for groups in which the actors have learning disabilities. In part the director's methods and interests will help to create a 'house style', another aspect of theatre-making that is essential as part of a professional stance. Whilst a large number of the devising companies discussed in the previous chapters did away with directors and other specific roles in a drive towards the democratisation of the theatrical process, many later returned to more delineated functions. In doing so their house styles also changed direction, since the ways in which we choose to make theatre will inevitably drive or shape the work. Some theatre practitioners have commented retrospectively on how a lack of defined roles may have its downsides. For Nabil Shaban of Graeae, 'The danger with a devised piece was the attempt or desire to please everyone, and the attempt to give everyone equal parts, resulting in a homogenous piece.'[1] Claire Grove of Women's Theatre Group has also spoken of the way in which the attempt to consider everybody's views on every aspect of a work created 'a sort of gap in the middle of the group of people that was the play'.[2]

With actors with learning disabilities there is another factor to take into account: a complete lack of direction or total breakdown of defined roles has the potential to cause anxiety in those members used for the most part to being aided and directed – by teachers, carers and parents, for example. When working with actors with learning disabilities the theatre director must be aware of how easy it is to 'control' the work or impose methods or ideas on the actors, who may not have the ability or confidence 'to answer back'; nevertheless the director still has a crucial role to play in shaping the aesthetic and this is one which, given the lack of verbal 'dialogue' within the group, brings with it a significant responsibility. The director must remain aware that even where they think they are not imposing a style – in employing a completely open-ended approach, for example – they are still to an extent driving the direction of the work through their choices. An 'open' and seemingly democratic approach, for example, will not be to everyone's liking and people with learning disabilities who feel insecure when they do not understand the boundaries, such as people on the autistic spectrum, may find the uncertainty or vagueness of an abstract and flexible approach too uncomfortable.[3] The crucial issue is not to forego 'directing' but simply to remain aware; stylistic differences will occur in any theatre company and will be derived in part from the director and in part from the actors. What is crucial is that everybody knows where they stand, and feels comfortable with this arrangement, in order to begin to work collectively.

There are a number of starting points that will be employed in the early stages of devising a piece of theatre. These include a more specific use of 'props' or objects and a more intentioned use of music than that discussed in the previous chapter – the company might also draw on images or visits to different sites. The most important aspect of a starting point is that it provides a focus that is external to the group, an expressive stimulus with which the whole group may engage, even though each actor will respond differently. The aim is to find ways in which to begin to draw out the individual creativity of the group members. When moving on from the 'warm-up', which we looked at in the last chapter, it can be enormously helpful to find ways of moving seamlessly into the developing work.

This is important for two reasons. First, so as not to lose the energy and focus that has been generated but instead to channel it into something specific. Second, this approach avoids a return to self-consciousness. Setting up a scenario with a verbal (and cerebral) instruction (e.g. 'What we're going to do now is...') always brings with it an expectation and consequently a fear of failing to meet that expectation. It is preferable instead to move beyond the warm-up without breaking the focus. There are a number of simple ways to do this. Some require no additional external stimulus at all, insofar as other members of the group are already 'external' to the individual. Working simply with the people in the room, the director might suggest that one person joins another person: immediately an interaction has been set up. What the actors then choose to do in that situation, how they interact, is anybody's guess; the important thing is that the director has moved the scenario on from the warm-up and that the company are now making theatre. The actors might wonder momentarily what is expected of them but if the preparation work has been properly absorbed, they will know that they are free to create whatever comes spontaneously to them. They will also know that it will not be judged. Taking this further, one might begin to play with numbers of people – three people in a space, rather than two, creates a very different dynamic. Swapping one person with another again brings a different 'energy' into the situation, so that the remaining person changes in response to the new person. Such interactions require nothing more than the group members themselves, yet already we have begun to move on from individual warm-up into group dynamics. We have begun to make drama – since people and their interactions are at the heart of the dramatic moment.

Many practitioners find games a useful starting point but, as we have noted in the previous chapter, one needs to be aware of the danger that these may impose an expectation on the participants of a certain response or take them on a very specific emotional journey. It is also important to sense whether those involved in certain games or exercises are merely 'doing as they are told' and hence faking the interaction. 'Trust' games, for example, so frequently used to build a supportive atmosphere for authentic interaction, are all very well. Yet how often do the 'partners' who have demonstrated that they trust each other or built rapport in the studio then avoid eye contact out of embarrassment when they pass each other in the corridor? It may be more appropriate, and less time-consuming, to go straight for exploring eye contact itself.

For people with learning disabilities (especially the more severe conditions) there is a further factor to bear in mind. Many classic 'theatre' games depend on the element of competition. In our experience actors with severe learning disabilities tend not to respond to competition, perhaps due to lack of self-esteem (and therefore fear of failure) or simply not understanding the concept of competition itself. Instead simple interactions can often be the most profound. A rudimentary 'game' that has been developed as a result of working with actors with learning disabilities is that of 'eye contact'. Quite simply, in any number of formats (in pairs, with the group in a circle, standing at opposite sides of the room and so on) the director encourages the individual to make eye contact with someone else and to maintain eye contact as the participants move closer or further away from one another, changing directions, levels or completing different tasks. It is remarkable how few of us are comfortable being stared at and how rarely actors genuinely look at the person they are playing opposite. But when done simply and with integrity this most simple of exercises can make for intense and touching interactions. Starting point number one: you always have the people you are working with – work with what you have.

When it comes to introducing an additional, external element, for actors with learning disabilities (or indeed with any group of actors willing to respond to a new and perhaps less structured approach) music and objects become more than just props. And they can be introduced in ways that avoid justification or explanation. Crucial to our whole approach is to keep verbal instructions to a minimum and we aim to run whole sessions without recourse to verbal cues. We have already discussed the ways in which words can dupe us and serve to close down the authentic encounter. Whilst physical theatre groups, or even dance groups, work largely with the body, they nevertheless tend to fall back on discussion, conceptualisation, initial instructions and so forth, all of which might be seen to close down the possibility of authentic responses. The more open the environment for self expression, the more likely it is that one will receive a surprising gift of creativity, or genuine insight. After many experiences of trying to explain what we would like to see explored and finding our instructions ignored (through lack of comprehension), we have found it simpler and more productive to go with what comes naturally to the actors: to respond to them rather than expect them to respond to you. When a common understanding and rapport has been developed within an ensemble it is possible, and preferable, to suggest the development of an idea through a simple gesture or nod of the head, or to suggest the use of another stimulus by introducing it physically without explaining how it might be used. Again, this is about keeping the possibilities as open as possible, although it does rely on the actor and the director being 'in tune' with one another. If this has been achieved, through the methods and approaches described in the last chapter, an actor won't need to ask, 'What do you want me to do with it?' – he or she will just do what comes intuitively.

Objects

'A man walks across [an] empty space whilst someone else is watching him ... this is all that is needed for an act of theatre to be engaged.'[4] These are the now legendary words of director Peter Brook on the fundamental principles of theatre. Whilst this statement is not in doubt, we might ask how long that man can sustain the theatrical encounter before he feels the need to reach for an object or prop. Even when there is no object to hand this encounter may revolve around the man's lack of an available object and his subsequent desire for one. Our everyday actions are defined by the objects with which we come into contact. How long can we exist without interacting with an object? Consider the scenario. Stand alone in a room. In order to avoid a state of total inertia your mind will become restless. You will feel the need to do something. Before long you may be pacing the room, desperate to reach out and touch something, do something: to sit on a chair; lean against a wall; put the kettle on; light a cigarette; eat something; read the newspaper; turn on the radio; call somebody. Even the simple act of putting your hands in your pockets to relieve the boredom is an unconscious act of searching for something. You are literally trying 'to put your finger on' what it is that will release you from the anxiety of inertia. It is impossible for us to exist for long in isolation and in theatre, as in life, it is difficult to function without objects. If all the performer has to work with are words, then the performance becomes a form of live story telling or a poetry presentation. If the performance is non-verbal and the performer has only their body to work with, it becomes a mime show or a dance. To expand Brook's adage then, and at the risk of lessening its purity, 'A man walks across an empty space whilst someone else is watching him and, before long, he will interact with an object. This is all that is needed if an act of theatre is to be engaging.'

This is not to suggest that the use of objects is straightforward. How often is the dramatic potential of an object within the live encounter fully explored? Objects can all too easily become 'props' in the true sense of the word, too often employed in order to imbue a weak theatrical encounter with immediate realism or to create an illusory scenario – as such it can disguise an inauthentic or weak performance, quite literally by 'propping up' the theatrical illusion. In an age in which film relies for the most part on presenting vivid realism and in which digital technology goes even further by making 'reality' of our wildest imaginings (as with *Lord of the Rings*, *Harry Potter* et al.), the uniquely live and intimate nature of theatre as an art form places extra importance on the choice of 'props'. In the pared down world of theatre even greater attention should be given to deciding which objects are essential to the drama and which superfluous.

The choice of object by the director is of course an immediate imposition but this should be regarded in light of the director's role as facilitator rather than dictator. The key is to choose an object that opens up possibilities, rather than imposing one that offers only limited exploration. Where the theme of the piece has already been decided, this imposition will be inevitable. In preliminary rehearsals for a production of *Pinocchio*, for example, the authors chose to work with lumps of wood: what better starting point for a story about a wilful boy who is sculpted from a log? Yet the point of the exploration was not simply to use the wood to create the character of Pinocchio. It was to see if these lumps of wood might act as universal objects. In early rehearsals, guided by the inventiveness of the actors, the wood was 'brought alive', with the actors finding ways to present the 'inner spirit' of the log. Used in any number of ways the wood also gave to the piece a strong and coherent 'tactile' theme. Generally it is better to keep the objects unspecific, universal and even mundane; in short, to select objects that allow for the broadest possible range of responses – a plain white cloth, a stone or pebble, an empty cardboard box, a paper bag. It is possible to use heavily meaning-laden objects imaginatively but one needs then to work against what the rational brain suggests in order to truly explore the object's qualities. An umbrella is an interesting object but in order to move beyond its obvious function, we have to open our mind to its tactile and non-functional qualities. Approached in this way, an umbrella might suggest not rain but sensations of weightlessness, twirling, spinning, dizziness and flight. By beginning the journey in this abstract way rather than closing it down with a very literal object – or at least by employing a literal object in non-literal ways – the actors are enabled to delve deeply into their most intuitive and even unconscious responses: abstract objects stretch the actors and tend to produce more inventive work.

In Chapter I we mentioned the 'multi-sensory rooms' in special schools, full of technological wizardry designed to stimulate the senses of people with profound and multiple learning disabilities. The prevailing view in the early days within many companies making work for people with learning disabilities was that any 'props' that might be used in a production also had to be 'extraordinary' or at least 'artistic'; thus many hours were spent crafting special objects. In fact found, real and everyday objects have proved more significantly theatrical due to the very fact that they are, on the surface, ordinary and familiar. Through the process of theatre the mundane and ordinary can become magical. A workshop for a local school run by one of the authors, for example, consisted of filling the rehearsal room floor with autumn leaves; an entire session was spent exploring the young people's responses to them.[5] Previously we might have spent days cutting 'artistic' leaf shapes out of tissue paper and marvelling at the pretence and at the 'manufactured' responses from the kids; instead the ordinariness of the real leaves explored in the extraordinary setting of a church hall was what prompted a unique encounter.

Since objects require physical intervention of some sort, a strong justification for their use at an early stage of devising is that the group is immediately spurred into action and distracted from the concern of 'having to come up with something'. It is extremely valuable if the director (in the role of facilitator) considers the way in which an object is introduced into a scenario as this can radically affect the way in which interactions with that object ensue. It is also another example of the benefits of communicating without words. If an object is carefully and tenderly introduced into the space, the tone and mood of the work that arises will tend, too, to be considerate and tender. If an object is suddenly and unexpectedly catapulted into a scenario, the theatricality of the action will tend to draw out more energetic responses. How often, in a workshop setting, do we see a director or facilitator unthinkingly place a chair in the middle of the space whilst talking about the next exercise, when the dramatic impact of placing the chair in silence might in itself suggest a whole series of interesting encounters? If we are introducing a chair, how might we do it? Drag it along the floor, carry it with ease, trip over it, sit on it whilst trying to move it at the same time? Each approach suggests an opening for a different and unique dramatic scene. The way we introduce an object can be engaging, creative, inspiring, ideally liberating and above all, through its silence, theatrical.

There is absolutely no reason why these approaches cannot be used with any actor in devised work in order to begin to generate material. In fact, resisting the need to conceptualise or verbalise the proceedings and instead working intuitively undoubtedly produces more imaginative work by anybody willing to let go of their day-to-day responses and, for many professional actors, perhaps a large element of their training. For people with learning disabilities we have found this approach not just valuable but essential. Many people with learning disabilities are limited in their use of fine motor skills or hand–eye co-ordination. This can make the handling of objects challenging; consequently there is a greater sense of achievement when the individual successfully masters an object's use, especially if the person has been discouraged from handling objects because someone else, wanting to help or to avoid an accident, has always stepped in and done it for them.

Actors with learning disabilities also often appear to be open-minded about the possibilities of an object: what it can or should be used for; what it might alternatively become. This seems to be particularly prevalent with people with Down Syndrome, who often possess an ability to accept things however they are presented. Offer a person with Down Syndrome a banana and say it is a gun and they will likely take it and pretend to shoot someone. The opposite might be true of someone with autism. A common trait here may be a desire for logic and, although one might presume that this would be a barrier to inventive creativity, it is not necessarily the case that the person with autism lacks imagination (this surely comes down to what we mean by 'imagination' in the first place). Even the desire for order may be interesting, and someone with autism might handle an object in a very literal way with a peculiarly intense precision. This precision is in itself both important and expressive of that person's view of the world and contains within it a particular creative expression. Whether the actor is exceptionally literal and focused or, on the other hand, exceptionally open, to new interpretations, the key to the expressive potential of the act lies in the authenticity with which the performer engages with the object.

Objects are particularly important for those with profound and multiple learning disabilities – our work with such audiences relied on the importance of tactile communication within a narrative that was related to real-life experiences. Whilst it may still be some time before we can grasp how to work with people with very severe disabilities as professional actors, what such work makes clear is that for the interaction with an object to be more than mere physical stimulus, it needs to have a genuine artistic and dramatic significance. The object must be invested with meaning – any meaning – beyond its practical function. Objects can be 'containers' for meaning: why else would we treasure our own possessions, which are, after all, only inanimate matter? Why else would people become collectors? (In this respect the desire to collect, arrange and catalogue objects or to take objects apart, so prevalent in autism and Asperger Syndrome, may be seen as an enormously imaginative investment of meaning in the object.) For some of us, objects are treasured because of very specific associations or memories – yet for others the 'meaning' or import of the object is much harder to pin down, and it is this more expanded sense of meaning in which we are interested. The tactile nature of objects immediately engages the senses. More importantly, however, an object has the power to bypass cerebral or rational thought processes and to bring us in touch with our most direct and intuitive responses.

Music

Whilst the expressive potential and intimacy of our interactions with objects may not be obviously apparent until we truly examine them in the ways we have described, music is more widely noted for its ability to transcend controlled intellectual responses. Music has the power to reduce us to tears (how often, by contrast, do we cry in front of paintings?), to uplift us, to bring us down, or even to insinuate itself in our mind against our will. For these reasons music can be a powerful means of drawing out expressive potential. We have discussed the use of music in the early stages of group formation and in the warm-up. Music also plays a crucial part within the earliest stages of a devising process, though its function here – and the type of music chosen – will be rather different.

Music can be a crucial element in driving forward the creative process. It has the potential to help develop a narrative (understood as a sequence of images, actions and scenarios that combine to form meaning) and, like an object, can be the pivotal force behind an entire show. Especially where use of the spoken word has been rejected, music can become the language through which an ensemble 'speaks' and which, in turn, shapes its interactions. It should never be used simply as an 'accompaniment' to pre-existing work, however, to 'bolster up' the action or thoughtlessly to fill in the gaps between scenes. Whilst for many of the devised theatre ensembles discussed earlier, particularly those with an emphasis on non-linear, visual narratives, music is also crucial, it is often used to tie together various 'narrative' elements. For IOU, for example, 'Scenes are edited together, cut together abruptly or slid into one another. The music holds this non-narrative sequence together, the juxtaposition of familiar and unfamiliar instruments and styles is an integral part of the shifting atmospheres.'[6] We are interested here in music's potential to generate theatrical responses from the outset. Used in this way music can exist in a symbiotic relationship with the actors and their actions. It can fuel the imagination and the emotions, create atmosphere, focus and involvement, and allow for the performers' internal worlds to be externalised.

In using pre-recorded music the choice is crucial: whatever is used, the aim is to find music that has imaginative, emotional and narrative potential, which allows the actors to imagine new things, feel things in new ways and go to new 'emotional' places. We have found that music that contains no words, either spoken or sung, has more expressive potential. Lyrics can begin to define the scenario and therefore place limits on the imagination. It *is* possible to find music in which the lyrics act in dynamic or ironic counterpoint to the action but this already assumes a shared understanding of the lyrical content and, even where this understanding is shared by all members of the group, there is a risk of bringing musical 'baggage' to the process that begins to define or drive the narrative. The same can occur with a piece of classical music that, due to its use in a well-known film, has too many associations. The adagio from Mahler's fifth symphony, for example, will mean Visconti's *Death in Venice* to so many people that it cannot be used 'fresh' – only ironically. This is not a problem within the rehearsal studio if the actors themselves are not aware of the connotations but if this music is then carried over into the final work the audience will imbue the piece with unintended meanings. Contemporary popular and world music without lyrics is difficult to find but it works well because it seems to invite broader interpretation than a classical piece like Beethoven's Fifth Symphony, for example, which seems instead to ask us to devote ourselves to listening. Music with a dominant rhythm can be useful in encouraging an energetic physical response but at this stage is perhaps too prescriptive since the dominance of the physicality inhibits subtler, more emotional responses.

Wolfgang Stange of Amici Dance Theatre (a company that works with performers with and without learning disabilities) has developed a technique whereby he offers the group a choice of three pieces of music (simply numbered one, two and three) and, without telling them what they are, asks them to select one. This avoids the imposition of a particular mood on the group and ensures that the work that the music stimulates is entirely spontaneous. Equally, one actor might choose a particular track from a range of possibilities with which the company have been working. Or the director might choose a piece of music in response to what the company have been creating together, or in order to explore a particular aspect of the work that he or she senses needs developing. Alternatively, if one wishes to introduce a specific emotional narrative or journey (because the piece requires it) a sequence of tracks can be edited together with the express purpose of suggesting a narrative. If it is introduced in the right way the interpretation by the performers will still be spontaneous and, ideally, will produce some surprises.

At this stage of the process, the use of music begins to broaden from being primarily a stimulus for the actor's expression of his or her individuality and creativity to including the possibility that music can already contain emotion, narrative and even characters that the actor must seek to express, embody and interpret. In this way the actor sets up an internal dialogue with the music. To an extent the music contains an already delineated route, but nevertheless the right music is open to all sorts of possible interpretation and this is where the choice of music becomes crucial. It must have emotional depth but it does not need to have a rigid emotional clarity. For example, the same piece of music – the second movement of Philip Glass's *Violin Concerto* – has been used with actors to explore a number of different narratives: the sense of losing something precious and becoming distraught; the sense of being lost in a strange place and then finding a source of great joy; even to interpret the first meeting between Titania and Bottom in *A Midsummer Night's Dream*. All of these narratives are potentially contained within the music and can be unearthed through the individual and collective creativity of a company.[7]

Another approach is to bring in a musician to work alongside the actors in the studio – here the actors must be allowed to affect the music as much as the music affects the action. In this respect the musician must be highly skilled at improvisation and content to be guided by the work of the actors rather than imposing a mood or rhythm on the work. In all cases the music will have different meanings for and provoke different responses in each individual actor and under different circumstances. At the very earliest stages what is important is that the devising of a piece remains a dynamic two-way process in which the more that is discovered about the imaginative, emotional and narrative possibilities, the more the piece is allowed to shift and develop. The music might be changed to fit the piece – or vice-versa, with the existing sequence adapted and shaped as the narrative develops. Alternatively the music used as an initial starting point might be abandoned altogether, with a composer brought in at a later stage to construct music that better connects with the narrative that has begun to emerge.

In many ways these approaches to the use of music are no different to the ways in which it is utilised within the dance studio. Nevertheless the differences between theatre and dance are important. For us, despite a strong physical focus, we remain interested in the use of traditional theatrical devices – plot, character, situation, gesture, mime and so on, as well as in highlighting the unique bodily expression of the performer, which is often superseded within conventional dance formats at the behest of the choreographer. Because there are superficial similarities between dance and physically driven theatre (primarily because it is non-verbal and the narrative is often abstract) this can invite misunderstandings on the part of the audience, especially where the performers do not have the conventional 'movement skills' of professional dancers. This is an issue for any performer not trained in dance but who chooses to work in a physical or crossover performance style. The real focus of such work should be the individuality of physical expression rather than the control and technical skill of choreographed movement. If achieved authentically, with the director as 'choreographer' working entirely from the range of physical expression and its possibilities as offered by the actor, the audience is more likely to accept it on its own terms.

At the same time, work which relies on 'world class' music in performance by actors who are not professional dancers also sometimes invites criticism for precisely the opposite reason, with the suggestion that such music creates impressive effects *at the expense* of the performances. This ignores the interplay between the actors and the music, however: good quality music should simply invite better quality responses; poor quality music will fail the actors in their physical expression. The closer the connection between what is seen and what is heard, that is, between the actors and the music, the better the work will be, with the music seeming to emanate from the action, to be intrinsic to it rather than a decorative accompaniment. For some members of an audience, of course, such work may not have a strong appeal – many people who are not accustomed to 'tuning in' to a performance that is both visual and aural also find dance difficult to appreciate.

Perhaps instead this physically driven work has parallels with the best performances of the silent screen. Contemporary film scores can often be useful as starting points in the early stages of development in devised theatre work. The fundamental difference is that within the medium of film, the scores for the most part are written after the work of acting has been done and are based on the final cut. Here we are suggesting its use as a starting point for creative expression. In silent film, the accompanying music would have been provided live at each performance. Whilst it is unlikely that the silent screen stars worked to music in rehearsals, nevertheless, without verbal dialogue to rely on, these actors were compelled to express emotional meaning primarily through the body. It is notable that Louise Brooks was originally trained as a dancer and her performance in Pabst's *Pandora's Box* of 1929 is largely movement-driven. Yet this movement is still in the service of a conventional narrative. We are not suggesting that the work under discussion is synonymous with silent movie acting, but where the silent movie is perhaps most similar is in the experience of the audience, who 'receive' a performance in which silent action is mirrored by the emotional narrative of the music – in silent cinema, as interpreted by the musician. The sort of work we are discussing is neither dance nor, strictly speaking, 'physical theatre'. In dance, in physical theatre – and also to a large extent on the silent screen - significant conceptualisation tends to take place alongside and in between the physical work. For our work, the response to the music should be less conceptually sophisticated and more intuitive.

In discussing the importance of music within the devising process, we are not advocating notions of 'musicianship', although there is nothing to stop the performer exploring the creation of music themselves if it comes from an impulsive expression. This can either be vocal or through the use of instruments. It is an old adage that there is no such thing as a 'tone deaf' person; what prevents a person from confidently singing, for example, is not a lack of technique or natural ability but a series of emotional blocks and degrees of self-consciousness that prevent true engagement with the source of their potential voice. (It is possible for a person to be technically proficient in 'mimicking' a singing voice not necessarily their own; such proficiency can undermine the ability to actually sing authentically.) Likewise we are interested in encouraging the self-belief and expressive potential of the actor, enabling him or her to relax, to listen, to sing – if he or she is so inclined – to open up to intuitive responses and to forget any inhibitions or perceived limitations. We return to the issue of authenticity. By creating the right supportive working environment (often achieved through the 'warm-up' as described) it is possible for the most vocally inhibited performer to 'sing' from the 'soul'. As with some traditional folk or blues singers, the sound that is produced may not be of a technically high standard, yet few fail to be moved by the passion and emotion expressed through such a song. Ideally, one would take this raw creativity and develop it with practice and technique – it is more important, however, that the performer has found an authentic means of expression as a basis for theatre. In order to support this, it is possible to take sounds that have been created in the warm-up and turn them into a song, or begin to expand them into new words (from 'B' or 'bah...' to 'bath', for example), which in itself begins to suggest a different environment and another possible starting point. Dislocated words placed together can also make a poem that, in turn, may lead to the creation of a still image or sculpture to be brought to life through drama.

The creation of live music by the actors themselves might involve something as seemingly simple as playing an instrument that they have never played before. Percussion instruments such as drums or shakers are obvious examples and can be used to invite more inventive responses. They also, rightly or wrongly, bring with them fewer pre-conceived notions about the 'correct' way in which they should be played and so can be quite freeing for anyone who does not consider themselves a musician. A more adventurous approach (and here we might advise a good insurance policy!) is the creative exploration of a more technically challenging instrument such as a cello, grand piano or tuba (to take just three examples from the classical western range of instruments – one could equally consider instruments from other cultures). The approach is similar to those we describe in the use of objects as stimulus, and the same problems of pre-conceptions apply – we all have an idea of how a grand piano 'ought' to be played, just as we all have notions of what a chair or umbrella is 'for'. If one can overcome these limitations and explore the instrument simply as an object that produces sound, an un-trained performer may yet produce outstanding and inventive pieces of music theatre.

To conclude, the use of music, or even simply sound, in the earliest stages of devising can range from the most basic of live vocalisations by the actors themselves to the use of pre-recorded music by highly respected composers to evoke expressive physical responses. What is important in all cases is that the actor feels able to bypass intellectualised reactions and simply 'feel the music'. This is the case for all actors prepared to work in this way and may be particularly useful for those working in physical theatre who wish to further limit verbal interventions, or for those in dance wishing to 'forget' their training, even momentarily, in order to reconnect with their natural physicality. The crucial point is that with actors with learning disabilities such a process seems to come naturally and it can be a reminder to us all of the fundamentally expressive nature of music.

The work of physical theatre groups, influenced by the training methods of Jacques Lecoq and others in Paris who were interested in reviving the mime and *commedia dell'arte* traditions, has much in common with the work currently being produced by actors with learning disabilities, and there are, doubtless, similarities with the methods described here. As with all other aspects of the work we are proposing, openness is everything: whatever is made, whatever comes about in the studio, must be allowed to happen organically. Labels such as 'physical theatre' close down the possibilities for each particular work and for future development. The work does remain physically driven, however, and music is one of the most important starting points for encouraging physical expression.

Places, Images and Other Starting Points

The range of potential starting points is infinite: places, images and other stimuli all offer the potential for generating theatrical material. We have concentrated here primarily on our own working experience of starting points – objects and music – though we have used others to a lesser degree. Awareness of environment, for example, can also be a fruitful starting point for making theatre. Opening ourselves up to new environments inevitably opens us up to new experiences and working with the actors in a new site can be a powerful way of generating intuitive responses. Many devised theatre companies have worked on-site with communities to produce site-specific theatre – where the site or environment is both the stimulus and setting for the piece. Major Road, based in Bradford, worked with students with profound disabilities in their highly visual and expressive piece *A Drop in the Ocean*, whilst IOU, Welfare State, Forkbeard Fantasy and Lumiere and Son have all produced site-specific work on different scales. Their aims vary: whilst Major Road were, and others continue to be, primarily concerned with the communities in which they are working and draw from the site issues relevant to that group of people, Lumiere and Son by contrast place the emphasis squarely on the quality of the final product. Here we are not suggesting that a new site need necessarily be the final setting for the work, just as an initial piece of music may not be used in the final performance but will give way to a completely different score during the devising process. As with all of the starting points suggested in this chapter, the primary aim is to provide an external focus to which the actors can respond and from which drama may begin to emerge.

Sometimes, however, a site can be overpowering and, like the use of objects, a simpler environment can, ironically, facilitate more interesting responses. A visit to a viaduct in France, with its impressive views of a disused railway track, a bridge, a valley and a tunnel left the actors overwhelmed rather than expressive: joining hands and singing a simple song in the echoing darkness of the tunnel at last produced the dramatic encounter that was the most genuine response to that site. It may be enough simply to go outside to the nearest piece of open ground to experience the sensation of being outside and feeling the elements. A simple walk could, on the other hand, prompt an entire narrative, not only in the strictest sense of producing a 'story' but, perhaps more importantly, in the sense of providing a narrative journey for the devising process itself. Real aspects of a journey – starting out with a strong sense of direction, for example, getting lost and downhearted, a mad scramble to the finish at the end – all these suggest an 'emotional journey', which can become central to a developing work. Again, bringing the external environment inside can prompt imaginative encounters, as we have seen in the case of autumn leaves. In another production, based on *The Tempest*, a major feature of the set was a pool of water. At various points this was used to great effect to re-enforce the elemental themes in the play.[8] The simple act of scooping up water in a cupped hand and listening to the dripping sounds transported the audience from the mundane surroundings of a school hall to an isle 'full of noises, sounds and sweet airs, that give delight, and hurt not'.[9] At another moment, Caliban's costume, dragged through the water and shaken at the audience in rage, produced an element of excitement and danger in keeping with the character's mood, and directly involved the audience in the action. Natural elements rather than mass-produced objects also have the power to override any attempt at pre-meditated research. It is also worth bearing in mind that 'anywhere' is a 'site' and that any site is able to provide a starting point if we are open enough to find it.

Images can provide another starting point or act as one of many. Again, this is not at all unique to ensembles with actors with learning disabilities and for obvious reasons has been a common starting point for those collectives stemming from visual arts backgrounds and interested in visual theatrical languages. The People Show cite an Edward Hopper painting, *Night Hawks*, as one of their starting points, whilst for Hesitate and Demonstrate (no longer practising), founded by Geraldine Pilgrim and Janet Goddard in 1975 (both trained in fine art), the entire devising process was constructed through a layered process of drawing and talking. Such a process differs from the one we are advocating, not least in the fact that lengthy discussion is unlikely to be fruitful with actors with learning disabilities, nor is it a part of the visual expression we are seeking to create, and images often still require a conceptual engagement that may be alien to many actors with learning disabilities. Nevertheless it does reveal how in theatre with a very visual focus, images can be as much a starting point as a literal idea: here meaning itself becomes visual.

We have suggested some potential starting points and talked in depth about those we have found most fruitful for creating theatre with actors with learning disabilities. Perhaps key to each stimulus is the fact that they appeal directly to the senses, and we have chosen to focus primarily on the tactile and aural. There are others: Figment Theatre, for example, have explored taste as a starting point for character work. Having tasted various foods while blindfolded, the actors translate their responses into character traits. Whatever starting points are chosen, the key is to be instinctive rather than intellectual.

In all these situations it is important to allow appropriate time for creative work to grow. Rose Myers of Melbourne's Arena Theatre has noted in another context that she likes 'to see what happens when people play a scene way beyond its natural end'.[10] Like the photographer who finally gets the right picture after the subject thinks the shoot has finished, sometimes the best material comes after the obvious ending. There is always more mileage to be had and it is as much about nerve as skill when a director allows an improvisation to continue past this point. It is equally important not to get 'precious'. The director must always be on the lookout for the right moment to find another stimulus, to prevent the emerging work from becoming stale or 'stuck' or self-indulgent. The director's job is to know when to intervene and when to refrain. This requires sensitivity to the situation and to the people with whom one is working, a sensitivity that can and must be developed on the part of the director. However it is achieved, having begun to generate responses, it is now important to begin to generate theatrical material.

8. Tasleem Hussain, Richard Ward, Kelvin Syme and Matthew Gosnay in *Scary Antics* by The Shysters. © 1999 Michael E.. Hall.

V

Generating Material, Character and Narrative

Practitioners with a background in devised and ensemble work will be familiar with the task of generating theatrical material from nothing. The approaches to theatre-making advocated in this book certainly have their basis in by now familiar devising processes rather than conventional script-based models, however they also differ from them in a number of significant ways. What seems to be unique to our approach is the extent to which the forms, characters, images and narratives are unearthed from within the actors rather than imposed externally, with the work being generated and progressed from and through the actor's embodied subjectivity at all points in the process. Such work is almost archaeological, with the material being 'excavated' rather than 'invented'; for us the play that will eventually be made already exists within the artists and actors and needs only to be unearthed. The processes of releasing buried emotions and elements of personality are not abandoned in the generation of material but nuanced and developed such that the final work *derives from*, but is not *about*, the actors themselves. This is also more than a collective rational decision to work on a particular theme or an issue of importance to all the group members. Instead we advocate reversing the theatre-making process, so that rather than training actors to embody characters, perform narratives and discuss themes, these characters, narratives and themes emerge organically from the actors' emotions and expressions. The work is not a simple performance of the personal. Nevertheless the connection between actor and character, life and narrative is certainly more profound than is generally the case.

Throughout this book we have emphasised, and will continue to emphasise, the organic nature of the approaches described. There are certainly phases in the process, which we have replicated for clarity in the structure of this book, yet the overall development remains fluid. This means that there is no clear or abrupt moment at which we cease to work with the actors' internal worlds and suddenly introduce a play based on what we have discovered and into whose parts the actors can be neatly slotted. This organic approach extends to the development of character and form, which are intertwined and arise in tandem: an exploration of character, for example, might inform further work on the narrative, whilst an emotional quality that is being expressed might lead to an exploration of style. This is why the preparation of the actor or, to put it another way, the development of trust between the actor and director, is crucial. Without this trust, effective expression of the actor's experience would not be possible.

When we speak of generating material, then, the sense of generation comes closer to the notion of the conversion of one form of energy into another than the idea of the production or creation of material 'from scratch'. The theatrical material is already there within the actors, lying in wait as impulses and emotions, in their imaginations and physicality, which we aim to creatively convert into gestures, characters, stories and images. Resisting the desire to force theatre to happen, we instead continue to find ways to unearth this 'sensory landscape', to allow it to emerge and be made manifest through form. In this sense, though we prefer not to theorise or over-conceptualise what is after all an intuitive and 'illogical' process, the conversion of impulses into forms seems to echo that balance in theatre, discussed by Nietzsche, between the Dionysian release and the Apollonian drive towards meaning and image-making. The images unearthed also have much in common with the Freudian 'dream-work'; again, we do not mean this in the therapeutic sense but in the way in which dream manifests through a language of images or impulses already embedded within the psyche. This image-language or visual meaning will be discussed in more depth in the following chapter. What is crucial for us and what we seek to take further than is ordinarily the case is the transformation from the impulse to the manifestation. This is no arbitrary conversion but an archaeology of impulses that find their own forms; it is perhaps because we trust that the actors will be able to manifest these that we are able to advocate such an open-ended process.

Nevertheless not everything that emerges will present itself as workable. Whilst every emotion truly expressed is valued and valid, as with a therapeutic model, the difference here is that these emotions will be understood to be in the service of a piece of theatre. As such not all will be useful in relation to the final work. It is a matter of trial and error, with every emerging theme or idea being explored and tested on the floor. If the actors cannot work with a particular idea or motif then, for us, it is not worth pursuing. If it is not *real* for the actors, any work that leads from it will by nature be inauthentic.

Before discussing in depth the ways in which this generating process works in practice, it is worth noting the shifting role of the director in the devising process. Certain basic elements of the role remain the same throughout. We advocate being hands-on in the sense of not being aloof from the work on the floor, and hands-off in the sense of refraining from insensitive imposition. At this stage, however, and then again later when shaping the emerging material, the director's role begins to shift, with a subtle progression from almost complete immersion in the studio work to a more flexible position. From here the director is able to step into, and back from, the work as required. A new flexibility on the part of the director is necessary at this point in order to allow the work to develop without at the same time closing it down prematurely.

The Shifting Role of the Director

At this stage the director will still be working with the actors on the floor. From full involvement, working alongside the actors in warm-up work, he or she will begin to take a step back, subtly shifting from co-worker to a position from which he or she is able to 'provoke' or intervene in the proceedings. Since we do not advocate sudden announcements about the need to 'come up' with material, much of what begins to emerge at this stage will have led on from the explorations with music, image-making, objects and other starting points described in the previous chapter. As such, and in conjunction with new levels of confidence on the part of the actors, the process will be led very much by the actors' own explorations. Prompts must then remain simple, perhaps taking the form of a gesture (or a couple of words, if the group has not decided to eliminate the verbal element entirely), whose aim is to help to guide the development of a motif or point of interest. There will be subtly shifting levels of involvement, with the director taking a more internal or external role as appropriate. Working within the group and in semi-role, the director might simply alter an actor's position or viewpoint, perhaps gently prompting the actor to face in a different direction. He or she might also offer a single word or phrase at an appropriate point in order to consolidate the narrative that seems to be emerging in the improvisation. In doing so, it nevertheless remains important to try to 'sense' intuitively what is happening rather than 'seeing it' from a distance as a moving visual tableau. (There is certainly a place for this, however, during the later stages of rehearsal.)

This consolidation is important, despite our emphasis on allowing the actors to drive the work, since we need to be sure that the group as a whole is seeing the work in the same way. It is also important, especially in an ensemble's early days, precisely *because* the approach emphasises a lack of 'control' when it comes to improvisation and, especially, warm-up work. Having taken the method on board, the actors will be keen to uphold their responsibility not to control or dominate, so much so that they may struggle to move the work on from the abstract to the concrete. And it can be tempting not to take this step, even for the director, especially where a particularly beautiful or magical moment has been created. Yet it will fall to the director to break the spell if the work is not to become precious: there will be other moments, and the group must risk passing them by in order to begin to make something tangible.

By way of illustration, envision a scenario within an improvisation in which the group has begun to waft a piece of cloth and to make soothing sounds over the body of one of the other actors, who is lying down. The cloth has been laid over the actor and some sort of ritual is being played out that suggests to the director both that the person under the cloth is 'dead' and that the other actors are aware of this reading. The decision then might be to use this situation to explore 'death' as a theme. In order to consolidate the narrative the director needs, first of all, to ensure that everyone involved is conscious of the move into a more concrete scenario. Most importantly, but also more pragmatically, he or she will want to indicate to the actor under the cloth that, for the good of the drama, it is better that they do not suddenly 'come back to life'. Rather than breaking the atmosphere by stating overtly the direction the improvisation is taking, the director might simply introduce an interjection such as, 'He was a good man. We are sorry that he is no longer with us.' This affirmation could equally be achieved through an appropriate gesture, if the group has developed a code for working within a completely non-verbal framework.

Such an interjection also suggests to others involved in the improvisation that they might develop the narrative further. The actors may wish to 'reminisce' about the character and from here begin to develop a storyline. This would of course take the improvisation into the verbal realm and in doing so it would temporarily lose some of its more interesting and unique physical qualities. And then again, it is also the director's duty to be aware of how much mileage is being generated within this verbal section, in order to gauge when the moment is right for moving the scenario on again. The director might then give a prompt such as 'no more words' (or, alternatively, make a gesture or sound to suggest the same instruction) in order to return the actors from acting primarily 'with the mind' and back into spontaneous physical creativity. In sensitively guiding the work forwards, the director is not choreographing but certainly orchestrating the shifting dynamic of the improvisation. He or she must both respect and enable this dynamic movement, this sense of shifting back and forth, which is the key to the creative process.

Nevertheless, even within this dual position of internal/external involvement, the director will still be rather more embroiled in the work than is typical, at least in conventional theatre. Due to the conventional hierarchies and set roles inherent to mainstream theatre practice, but also to the fact that many people with learning disabilities will have carers and others who have intervened for them, those new to such work may worry about the lack of a secure hierarchy. Will this be discomfiting to the actors? In fact, in our experience, it is the non-disabled performer who at first finds the lack of clarity most confusing. If an actor is used to the standard structure of read-through, plotting, character development and so forth, with the director sat behind a table giving occasional notes and prompts, it can be unsettling to have the director in amongst or even joining in with the actors. This may be especially unsettling at this generating stage, when one might expect even the most experimental and involved director to have resumed their place in the director's chair.

A director new to this approach might also be concerned: if they are too closely involved in the unveiling action, how will they be able to judge objectively the quality of the work that is developing? Yet we have found that, both for actors with learning disabilities and many non-disabled performers, the more fluid approaches and an egalitarian atmosphere in fact make for greater creativity. If the actor sees that the director is prepared to take risks and expose themselves to vulnerability, they are also more likely to drop their defences and reach into themselves more creatively and authentically. Perhaps one might argue that it should not be a requirement, as part of the director's role, to put professional actors at their ease. But we are exploring new territory here and with this new territory must come new models of practice.

It is interesting in this light to refer back to those collaborative ensembles discussed in Chapter I who, after an initial non-hierarchical period, often returned to more traditional roles and whose members have spoken about the downsides of complete collective collaboration. There are times when a creative process needs a voice of authority to consolidate the direction of the work and this voice may be more easily heard when the director is at one remove from the process. Yet for actors with learning disabilities a democratisation of the creative process is crucial. Too often in their day-to-day lives, due to the misapprehension that they would be incapable of discovering something for themselves or of stating a personal preference, they have been told exactly what to do. Given time and space, and a secure working environment, anyone can develop the confidence to give expression to their inner instincts.

It may be that the provision of such a supportive environment will become less necessary over time. As people with learning disabilities are increasingly respected and given access to good education and considered working conditions, their confidence inevitably increases. The next generation of actors with learning disabilities may prove more comfortable with a traditional hierarchy, and future directors may not have to take on to the same extent this supportive, facilitating and empowering role, especially if the actors have received previous formal training. The work under discussion is pioneering – we can only guess at how it might develop.

Another role of the director – that of mediator or 'interpreter' – also starts to come into play at this stage in the devising process. This aspect of the role comes fully to the fore in the 'editing' stage described in the following chapter, when the director begins to frame, shape or even conduct the emerging work. Here it is the director's job simply to ensure that communication is effective. But it is also important at this early stage, in which he or she must begin to translate the 'world' of the play that is beginning to develop, to facilitate the transition from pure self-expression to that of communicating ideas theatrically. In principle this is no different to the traditional work of the director, although it can differ in three important aspects.

First, the sort of work under discussion has a more abstract, imagistic, emotional quality than conventional improvised drama, especially that which stems from a pre-determined concept or issue. As such it will tend to rely more heavily on an 'interpreter' who, involved yet at one remove, is able to begin to 'read' the emerging visual and sensory narratives and images. Second, in the quest for authenticity, it is essential that reliance on artistry to cover over a weak performance is identified and if at all possible eliminated (regardless of whether or not the actor has a disability). Especially since the focus of the work is on the individual, as opposed to the creation of spectacle, and without wishing to fall back on the false realism of naturalistic dialogue or elaborate stage sets, the actor's performance in such work is placed even more clearly under the glare of the spotlight. Ironically, an actor is often the last person to realise that their performance is inauthentic. Any seasoned director should be able to see through a forced or affected performance. (This is also little different to the 'talent' spotter who senses the grains of authenticity in an unpolished, untrained singer and who, equally, spots the artifice that prevents authenticity in an apparently more polished performance.) It is also made easier by having got to know the actor first. All theatre work can contain devices, intentional or not, such as emotively manipulative dialogue or action that can disguise this recourse to artistry. With the type of work under discussion it is more obviously exposed. The role of the director as mediator therefore takes on an extra significance.

Finally, the role of mediator takes on a particular importance because of the ethical issues of working with actors who may not have the same ability to voice a dislike of what they are being asked to do. Nor will they have a clear idea of how this work might appear to an onlooker. The director must ensure that the actor is comfortable with the work proposed and, as we have highlighted elsewhere, the integrity of the director is paramount. The best the director can do is to remain alert to the issue; ultimately there will be no moral arbiter. Perhaps a simple test is to ask, 'Would I be prepared to do this myself? Would I be comfortable asking a non-disabled performer to do it?' and then factor in some allowances based on personal knowledge of that individual – without at the same time succumbing to the fear of challenging the individual or of 'dumbing down'. It is interesting to note that despite a lack of eloquent verbal articulation, an actor with a learning disability is likely to be perfectly capable of expressing resistance if asked to do something with which they are uncomfortable – through a simple refusal to participate, for example. So whilst on the one hand there is clearly a need to remain aware of the potential for exploitation, it might in fact be the case that actors without disabilities, perhaps in awe of the director, are more rather than less likely to participate in theatre that makes them uncomfortable. This offers both a reminder and a warning: actors with learning disabilities will neither be pushed nor patronised. Likewise such vigilance should be a reminder to all directors about their responsibilities to the actors with whom they work.

A careful balance, then, needs to develop between the director's and the actors' creativities. These are the two faces – or forces – of creative expression at play in the devising process, and it is probably at this stage that they are most closely entwined. They can also, at times, be contradictory. The director must be careful not to push his or her own vision onto the actors, no matter how illuminating or inspired it might seem to be; the question of how to maintain authenticity in a collaborative context is one that all theatre practitioners making ensemble work will have encountered. At the same time he or she is of little use to the company as a blank canvas and the personal creativity of the director remains crucial. In effect he or she must become the 'conceptualising' element in an actor's development, whilst at the same time not allowing this use of concept to become overbearing. The director must be able to 'get inside the actor' and understand the acting process, rather than being overly concerned with its external appearance. How otherwise can he or she understand what the actor is capable of, or encourage him or her to push the work to its limits?

Generating Material

Since our process is as organic as is possible, in the early stages of generating material the group will be working primarily with whatever the actors intuitively offer up. Much of the work at this stage is about taking these 'offerings' and exploring ways in which to build on them and allow them to develop. Most practitioners with a background in devised theatre will be used to the process of generating material through improvisation. Alongside this, we continue to place emphasis on expressive emotional release stemming from the early explorations of the actors' inner worlds. This is because, for us, the early emotional and physical work is more than just preparation; it is also the source of the work itself. The most interesting work comes when an actor unearths something new or hidden about themselves and the personal transformation of the actor is also the fuel that drives his or her performance. Phelim McDermott of Improbable Theatre has spoken of improvisation being

> about the excitement of seeing someone go over an edge. One person puts someone else on the spot and says, sing a song and the person goes, 'oh I can't' and then they attempt it and the attempt is thrilling because there's some growth in that.[1]

It is this growth that we continually seek and which is the basis of the theatre we are interested in making.

It therefore remains the director's role to challenge the actor to explore new internal territories. Nor is such exploration specific to actors with learning disabilities – Glenda Jackson, for example, has spoken of her need to discover something new about herself in each new role, and in many ways this is synonymous with the process of acting defined by Stanislavski. For us this is rarely at the service of an existing role, however, and any characters that are created will be rooted in those aspects of the actor's own personality that are unearthed and embodied. Like the work of performance art and other early crossover forms, we are interested in *presentation* rather than *re-presentation*.

When an actor discovers and releases an aspect of themselves that has previously remained hidden or, at least, has been disavowed as 'unacceptable', 'inappropriate' or simply not fitting the person's public persona, a powerful theatrical performance can be the result. This might be an unacknowledged aggressive streak or, conversely and less spectacularly, a new calm or centred-ness in a usually boisterous or edgy individual. This is also apparent, on occasion, in mainstream work – sudden and unexpected transitions in role type (e.g. a comedy actor who produces an astonishingly authentic and sincere performance in a serious role) involve, we would suggest, a profound shift in the actor as a person as well as performer.

In doing this the actor recognises and acknowledges an essential but repressed aspect of who they are and, in displaying it on stage, is empowered to embrace this unknown or 'forbidden' trait within a safe environment. More importantly, in theatrical terms at least, they are also able to transform or sublimate it into a creative act through its 'physicalisation' in a role or character. For the psychoanalyst Jung, such unknown elements of the persona make up the 'shadow', those aspects of the person which, deemed unacceptable or ill-fitting, are rejected by the individual. For those with learning disabilities, whose behaviour will have encountered intervention and approbation on many occasions, this shadow, one might imagine, can be particularly weighty. It can also, once explored, produce profound theatrical material.

On the other hand, working from the physical inwards rather than the other way round can also unearth unknown aspects of a person. So, relating back to the 'Walk My Walk' exercise discussed in Chapter III, an unusual posture, or focus on a specific body part, such as the hips, might create a different way of walking. This might in turn translate into a pushy, thrusting character type. This is especially interesting if the actor is normally meek, mild-mannered or humble. Again the use of music might elicit a particular bodily response or gesture that can translate back into a new emotion. This is not about mimicry or comedy (though the results may well be very funny) but about the embodiment of a new persona or buried aspect of one's personality accessed through physicality. We will return to this in relation to characterisation.

This sense of embodiment can also be used in developing spatial memory. Despite the assumption that people with learning disabilities have poor memory skills, this in fact refers to a particular form of memory – rote learning – which is the basis for mastering sequences of words, spelling and numeracy. There are other types of memory, however, and the ancient mnemonic technique called the 'method of loci' is one that drew on bodily, spatial and visual rather than mental sequencing capacities. Here the person walked repeatedly through a series of spaces or 'loci' (sometimes called a 'Memory Palace'), in which fragments of text, mentally translated as striking visual images, were located in the imagination. It is possible, if one wishes to do so, to help memorization of lines by mapping out the physicality of a scene first and then repeating the movement sequence whilst feeding lines into it at key points. This highlights the validity of spatial memory which, in our experience, can be exceptional in actors with learning disabilities, who are often able to accurately replicate a piece of theatre that has been mapped out internally in a completely new and open environment. In one extreme example a group of actors on their first tour were able to translate a piece designed for performance indoors to a space marked out on a beach and using only the most essential props. One might assume that an actor with a learning disability would be 'thrown' by being asked to reproduce a performance in a completely different environment; our experience suggests otherwise. Techniques used for their own sake are to be avoided, since it is all too easy to exchange one form of training method or dogma for another. Nevertheless in work that is driven primarily by the body such heightened awareness of spatiality is inevitably useful.

Proceeding organically from the warm-up and early exercises not only endorses the authentic performance element but also smoothes the transition from 'play' to 'making a play'. The seeds of narrative, character and form are found within even the smallest, most formless or seemingly meaningless gesture. The director need only begin to 'read' these gestures – which is not the same as 'reading into' them. The latter implies a heavy-handed and usually flawed analysis of a possible 'meaning'. Instead the director works with the gesture, teasing out of it physical meaning (rather than conceptual meaning) and aiding the actor in its development. The director must at once be aware of an actor's feelings and what he or she is trying to communicate. Unlike dance, in which the dancer might execute a movement that elicits an intended emotion from the audience without, necessarily, 'feeling' that emotion, the movements elicited from experimental work have no repertoire or stock motifs on which to fall back. It is crucial therefore for the director to tease form out of the true and authentic gestures that are offered up openly in the studio.

This rooting of the work in the actors also promotes a particular approach to improvisation. Because of the subtleties involved, the director, as we have suggested, must be prepared to run improvisations longer than is usual, to sense when something has not fully played out or requires further stimulus. Sometimes an exploratory process will go on for a long time with little appearing to happen;

the warm-up, for example, might run for an hour before the situation shifts and the actors begin to reach into themselves creatively. The director must also be willing to jettison a particular plan for the day's events. Again, preciousness is fruitless in this context: an actor with a learning disability will make it clear within minutes of entering the studio if he or she is unable to take or is uninterested in taking a particular route that fails to reflect his or her own emotions at that time.

We have talked at length about our belief in keeping verbal instruction and analysis to a minimum. This extends to the improvisation period. Instead of recording (actually or mentally) the results of a particular improvisation and attempting to replay it precisely, we advocate identifying the seeds that generated the emotional scenario as a potential key for unlocking a similar emotion again. This is not a form of rehearsal but rather a process of creative development in which an original and perhaps simple idea can be drawn out and expanded by the full ensemble, even with an actor who might not end up playing the part explored. The piece will be physically elaborated, nuanced and detailed, understanding developed, memory enhanced, and the full meaning of a physical or sensory act explored. Returning to the piece, what will be replicated is the 'feeling' of a text and not the text itself. The feeling is where the forms are generated; too immediate a response to the forms themselves (in terms of trying to replicate a movement that worked well before, for example) will close down the authentic encounter in which the movement had been generated in the first instance. It is better then to return to the emotional texture of the work, or even to begin to move on from that point. This is an embodied way of working in which impulse, emotion and affect are allowed to avail themselves of their own appropriate forms, and in their own time, rather than having external forms foisted upon them. Analysis can block this passage back to the creative impulse. Repetition instead works through the generative impulse, layering nuance upon nuance until the form has 'found itself'. In this sense it is a poetic rather than conceptual process, a bodily semiotic rather than Symbolic way of seeking and expressing meaning.[2]

Character Development

By rooting the work in the bodies of the actors, we propose an approach to character development that is, again, organic. As we have suggested, characters emerge from within the bodily style of the actor, so that they are 'sensed' rather than 'devised' or invented. What is also, perhaps, unique to the work we describe, and which stems from this relationship, is the extent of the connection between the actor and character, with characters being embodiments or elaborations of aspects of the individuals. We talked in Chapter II about the fact that actors with learning disabilities may not fully comprehend the notion of characters as entirely divorced from themselves. They may also not be fully aware of a character's clear place within an overall work, that is, the way in which a character informs the piece as a whole, although they will certainly be aware of the ways in which a particular character acts in relationship with others.

This approach to characterisation calls into question the very notion of 'acting', just as the performance artists and experimental ensembles discussed previously blur the line between acting and 'action', performance of other and performance of self. The work we are advocating does not presume to present individuals *as they are* on stage: this, after all, would not be acting. Nevertheless each character will embody and perhaps magnify an aspect of the actor's real self within any given role. We would not expect, or even wish to encourage, work in which a naturally happy or joyful actor was forced to present (or re-present) the external appearance of an unhappy or miserable character. Equally we would not present this happiness unmediated or uncharacterised and call it theatre. And it may be that a seemingly happy person is, in fact, disguising a deep-rooted unhappiness; the release and embodiment of this unhappiness would then be revelatory both as theatre and on an individual level. Generally, character is too often described with words and not simply inhabited.

Inevitably, the 'personality' of the actor will shine through any great performance – this is true of all actors and of all types of acting, from the mainstream to the avant-garde. Perhaps actors with learning disabilities, due to a differing relationship to the processes of socialisation, have a unique ability to allow themselves to both inform and shine through any given performance – what we have attempted to describe as an un-self-conscious authenticity. The audience invariably respond to this. Equally, the actor must also learn to utilise their own unique nature or charisma whilst striving to transcend their habitual personas. We do not support the notion of the actor as an empty vessel and seek instead to encourage a theatre that roots the work in the individuality of the actor. Yet this actor must consistently attempt to grow and expand their range and the director must also strive to help them achieve this. Furthermore in this context there is a particular challenge: many people with a learning disability have a pronounced physicality and, at first, audiences may struggle to see beyond this to the subtleties that the actor brings to the performance *within* this particular bodily style. This is another reason why continued exposure of work by actors with learning disabilities is crucial.

Form, Theme, Narrative

If we agree that the worldview of a person with a learning disability may be 'different' to that of a person without, then we need to unearth, or allow to evolve, the forms through which these differing 'ways of seeing' might be embodied. (It is beyond the scope of this book and indeed our interest – since we are not concerned with labels – to question how much of this difference is attributable to the disability and how much in relation to others' perceptions of this difference *as* a disability). These are unlikely to be rigid, linear, clear-cut forms with attendant clear-cut and easily readable meanings. As such the aesthetic that emerges from such work tends not to be digestible in straightforward linear ways but instead takes on a poetic, sensory and imagistic nature that it is the director's job to 'translate' – without imposition or unnecessary intervention – for the audience. The particular task of translation will be discussed in depth in the following chapter.

Nevertheless the themes and motifs that emerge in such work are not so obscure as to be incomprehensible. They tend on the contrary to be universal, with themes such as anger at injustice, hate and love, guilt and forgiveness all coming to the fore. These might present themselves in subtle ways, which can then be elaborated in physical work and re-workings. An actor's ability (as a person) to remain calm and detached but then to suddenly explode in anger might be translated or embodied – and even exaggerated – such that the particular actor is able to take on the role of a very violent character. This actor will not be a violent person but will nevertheless be able to channel his or her latent aggression into a dramatic performance. Equally, where an actor feels a keen sense of injustice, he or she might be able to feed this into a character in a quite opposite sense. Instead of taking on the role of a person who has had injustices perpetrated against him or her, the actor might instead be able to articulate the irrationality of injustice via a particularly malicious or capricious role.[3]

The potential of an emotion to be explored via a character will become clear during the devising process and, especially, through the techniques of repetition and layering that we have described. Not all emotions expressed within the studio will find their way into a form, and certain themes will slowly emerge as extraneous, others essential. These will also change and develop as the actors grow in confidence. What is clear, yet again, is the extent to which this process will be driven by the actors themselves – and *should* be driven by them, in our opinion. Certainly the director and other collaborators such as stage set designers, composers and writers (to work with the group in producing snatches of poetic text, for example, rather than dialogue) will be able to feed ideas into the developing work. We recommend bringing these collaborators in as early as possible in the process to ensure a genuine group consensus. The key is to ensure true collaboration and never to allow a concept brought in externally to begin to determine, drive or even over-ride the development of the work. Just as the gestures, emotions and expressions of the actors in early improvisation work must be taken as crucial offerings, no matter how seemingly small, so too must the offerings of collaborators be taken on board – they are no less, but also no more, important.

At some point then, not only will certain recurring themes or motifs begin to emerge but they will also be necessary if the group is to start to create a theatrical language – even if this language is poetic and visual rather than literal, realistic and linear. We have talked about the usefulness of intervening by way of consolidating an emerging theme or motif. As the process develops this will become even more important and the point at which the general theme or loose storyline is openly consolidated and agreed upon is the turning point at which the 'play' – or 'piece of theatre' – has at last begun to find its form. It tends to fall to the director to initiate this consolidation and some actors will find this point of transition difficult or confusing. Boundaries begin to be set in terms of the relevance of material to the work at hand; inevitably the free-flow of early play and experimentation must at some point come to an end (still nevertheless rather later than is usual) if a coherent piece of theatre is to be made and performed. Furthermore this point also inevitably contains at least a basic element of conceptualisation that may be difficult for some people to comprehend, even if it is clear to the director, and it is often difficult to articulate a developing theme even for those with a full verbal armoury. If a consensus is slowly and organically reached, so much the better, since arrived at in this manner, all involved will feel a strong sense of ownership of the work that has fermented within the collaboration.

So the work, at last, begins to find its natural 'shape'. However, like a sketch, it will need filling out, detailing and sharpening. The material will also need 'editing' and framing. Inevitably the actors will be less directly involved in this next step, in part because such work requires a certain conceptual eye – albeit that this conceptualisation will be both poetic and intuitive – and in part because such close involvement in the generation of the material makes 'editing' difficult. The director must now be prepared to step fully into the role of mediator and, importantly, take up the position of the very first member of the audience.

9. Left to right: *Laura Sanchez, Robin Simpson, Peter Wandtke, Ben Langford and Vicki Hackett in* Pinocchio, *York Theatre Royal.* © 2007 Karl Andre.

VI

Visual Theatre: Structure, Narrative, Meaning

As in any creative process, through the development of the ensemble we will find ourselves in possession of a wealth of raw material. Like the first, formless draft of a novel, or the metres of celluloid from which will emerge the final cut of a film, this theatrical material will need to be shaped, structured and edited in order to give it a coherent form. The first editor of a novel is, of course, the author, with him or her taking a step back and beginning to arrange the themes, motifs and images and to refine the plot; in film the job will fall to the editor, in conjunction with the director, whilst the actors' work will already be complete. In text-based theatre, the actors' work assumes from its beginnings a precise structure, which is implicit within the narrative of the script. Devised theatre groups, conversely, take on a heavy workload, both generating and structuring material and, at last, performing the final work. For many devised theatre groups these various tasks may be shared equally amongst the members. When working with actors with learning disabilities, however, the director will be required to take on a primary role at this stage: he or she will be the driving force behind the way the work is structured. The director will also become the 'mediator' between the worlds of the play and of the actors and that of the potential audience.

In conventional theatre the director will have assumed this role at an early stage. From the outset the director will have brought to rehearsals a vision for the particular style or angle with which he or she wishes to invest or approach the piece, along with the writer's initial vision embedded in the script itself. There will be the designer's vision too, and perhaps that of the lighting designer. All these will have been influenced by the director's chosen approach to the work, however, whether traditional and in period costume or revisionist and contemporary. From the outset the actors will also have worked to translate this vision – a contemporary *Hamlet*, for example, might demand a focus on the spiky adolescent angst of the protagonist, whilst a more conventional angle will suggest a more classical delivery of the character's lines.

Devised theatre of the 1970s and early 1980s, as we have seen, eschewed these pre-determined scripts and concepts and, frequently, the role of director itself. For the most part the approaches we have described in this book are in line with the methods of early devised theatre, breaking down potential hierarchies through literal immersion in the studio work and doing away with 'conceptual' ideas in favour of organic and embodied on-the-floor approaches. The shaping process also has much in common with that of other devised theatre groups and especially those groups, such as The People Show, whose work is often categorised as 'visual theatre' or 'image theatre', and who explore primarily abstract and experimental forms.

The level of understanding required for processes such as editing, framing, conceptualising and structuring is generally difficult, however, for those with learning disabilities, for whom sequencing and the notion of 'cause and effect' are complex concepts. The director working with actors with learning disabilities will therefore have need to step back at this point into a more conventional role. Here, in fact, the traditional distinction between director and actor actually make sense for us: a truly embodied actor who 'feels' a part rather than 'thinks' it may not be best disposed to, at the same time, be objective about the work as a whole or to take on the work of the dramaturg. It may not be their forte, any more than the director's forte will necessarily be that of performing. We acknowledge the apparent inequality of a director without learning disabilities working with an ensemble of actors with learning disabilities, yet it has the potential to be a highly creative collaboration, a potential that lies at the heart of both of the authors' work.

It is interesting in this light to note that more recently formed ensembles producing visual theatre work (often now simply called 'performance' in order to signify its difference from text-based theatre)[1] for the most part employ directors as part of their ensembles. This may be part of a more general move to acknowledge that not everybody in a group has similar skills and that collaborative work can incorporate these different skills whilst still remaining collaborative – 'equal, but individual' – a stance that is highly appropriate to the general thrust of the work we propose. It may also be that image-led work particularly requires 'an external eye'. (Even People Show, who are insistent about their lack of an Artistic Director, have on one occasion brought in an external person to fulfil this role.)[2] Emma Rice of Kneehigh Theatre has also pointed out the way in which a division of labour can enable further freedom of expression on the part of the actors: 'Actors need to feel fearless and for them to feel fearless somebody has to look after them, to take care of them, and that's irrespective of any needs that we have.'[3]

For us the reason is quite simple: the actors' skills are in acting and not in conceptualising or directing. Even working with non-disabled directors, we believe that the work produced by actors with learning disabilities can look, feel and even *signify* differently. Access for people with learning disabilities to training in all aspects of the performing arts, including directing is, we recognise, totally inadequate. Our own contributions to redressing this imbalance have been in training actors rather than directors. It may well be that as more actors with learning disabilities gain professional experience and awareness they will also gain a better understanding of the skills required to direct. This in turn could result in work that looks and functions in new and as yet unimaginable ways.

The type of structuring, conceptualising and editing we are talking about is not entirely conventional, however, simply because the nature of the material is not conventional; nor, for us, is the end product. Working through the processes described in this book, a group of actors will have generated images, themes, recurring motifs and characters that are nevertheless also 'parts' of the actors; most importantly, they will not have discussed or generated a traditional linear storyline because the work will have been primarily emotional and embodied. It might be tempting at this stage to want to make these disparate theatrical 'units' cohere into a traditional play format. We would advocate against this, and shall discuss in depth the reasons later. When the aim is *not* to impose on the material a single reading or statement but instead to produce work whose meanings are multiple, fluid and open to interpretation, the editing required, then, will be of a very particular nature.

It is important to state here that this emphasis on fluid meaning might well be seen as a specific preference on the part of the authors: as directors we have preferences and house styles as much as anybody, and we admit to being more drawn to open-ended, experimental and poetic work. It might be argued that this is only one approach to the structuring of the material generated through devising theatre with actors with learning disabilities and that, since one is intervening in any case, one might as well intervene in such a way as to make the work immediately accessible to as wide as possible an audience. Certainly this might be attempted, especially if one feels strongly that the main benefit to the actors would be that of mainstream exposure, though it is difficult to say how far one could structure primarily non-verbal work into a traditional linear form. It perhaps comes down to a choice between 'fit' and 'remit' – between making final works that echo the nature of the material generated by the actors and, on the other hand, widening audience awareness of actors with learning disabilities. We are, without doubt, more interested in the former. But we would argue that this is not a vested interest, nor do we feel that it is simply one imposition out of a choice of impositions. In our experience actors with learning disabilities are not currently equipped to take on the role of dramaturg. It may be that few will ever be interested in taking on this role. This does not mean that we should not strive to structure the work in such a way that the actors are able to retain true creative ownership of the material as far as possible. Weighing a balance between the actors' needs and the importance of 'readability' from an audience perspective, the director, takes on, in effect, the task of translating the material.

The best translators convert one language to another not literally but with the intention of conveying the 'essence' of the original text. The art of translation is especially clear in poetry or other poetic writing forms where much of the meaning is embedded in a very precise combination of words, and which draws on their distinct sounds, rhythms, textures and connotations. Likewise since the actors' worldviews are not linear, not 'rational', not sequential and far from plot-driven, we feel it is important to produce work that remains true to these worldviews. We do not wish at this late stage to 'co-opt' their work for others, with the intention, also, of parading to the mainstream what actors with learning disabilities 'can do', parrot-fashion. This, for us, is not true creative equality since it has the potential to steal from the actors their authorial integrity. If the work is created, informed, guided and developed by the actors, and if it must take on a structure, why should this structure be alien to the people who made it and who will perform it? Some will question whether it is important for the actor to have this level of influence over a script or final play (although in devised theatre this is standard practice). Yet it would be a wasted creative opportunity not to utilise the particular qualities that the actors bring to the process. Pragmatically, we would also argue that a director will never get an authentic performance from an actor who is confused or alienated by the material that he or she is expected to perform. So in many ways it is a *fait accompli*. Aside from the issue of creative ownership and perhaps rather more pragmatically, having one's creative team fully engaged and utilised is surely good practice in any arena.

At the other extreme, of course, it might also be argued that in order truly to represent the worldview of the actors and reflect accurately the unique devising process, we should refrain from conceptualisation altogether. There is indeed an ethical justification for this. However in our experience the results, retained as they are, tend to be perceived as so 'experimental' as to appeal only to an extremely small and very enlightened audience. We have to weigh this against pragmatic and economic arguments since, as professional theatremakers, we must also consider our responsibility to an audience. Furthermore, we would be serving no one's interests in making work that very few people wanted to see and which confused rather than enlightened its spectators. We have emphasised the importance of not imposing on the actor a 'story' or structure simply because an audience will easily grasp it. It is equally important not to impose on the audience a piece of theatre that will leave them bored, bewildered, disengaged or even redundant, as can sometimes be the case with 'learning disabled theatre'. An actor with a learning disability can be a wonderful reminder of the free expressive artist. But this should never be allowed to become self-indulgent if the actor is to consider him or herself as a professional, and be regarded as such. We ask audiences to open their minds, to experience the work within its own frame of reference, but it must also maintain a level of internal integrity, coherence and readability if it is not to be confused with applied theatre. We will talk further about audience expectation and critical frameworks in the following, and final, chapter.

The role of the director, then, becomes that of a conduit or arbitrator between the worlds of the performer and audience. To an extent this arbitrating role is usual for the director, especially in traditional theatre where each actor often only studies in depth the scenes in which he or she appears – here only the director has an overall sense of the complete work. In the work we are proposing the actors will be involved in the creation of each and every role from the outset. Nevertheless an actor with a learning disability may be content to let the work remain abstract – perhaps because what is 'abstract' or 'abstruse' for others is completely coherent for the actor. This will remain difficult and unsatisfying for audiences (except perhaps for those who also have learning disabilities) and the professional actor must learn to appreciate how their work is perceived by others. Since the actor has expressed an interest in performing to a wider audience, they must also engage somebody else to translate this material for them, just as professionals in all walks of life – actors, singers, artists, businesspeople – frequently employ others – agents, PR people, stylists, financial advisors – to provide an objective overview. There is an additional factor here. Especially with actors with learning disabilities but, ideally, in all cases, it is also the director's role to support the actor in full self-expression whilst preventing them from 'crossing the line' into self-indulgence. The actor must be made to feel confident that they can trust the director implicitly with this task. As Emma Rice suggests, having this safety net is one less burden, and will allow the actor the space to take risks with their performance that they might not feel, under other circumstances, empowered to take.

What we propose, then, is still an equal collaboration, simply one in which the collaborators' roles are different. Having generated material, the director will want to begin to 'read' this material. In doing so, and with perhaps a commonly acknowledged theme beginning to emerge, he or she might suggest that a particular segment is reworked with a clearer emphasis or intention. Working in this way, the director might be disappointed to find that the result is a crude literal interpretation. In this process of translation it is tempting to accelerate the working process and impose themes and structures that the actors do not comprehend. They will inevitably make this known through their inability to grasp the shift in direction. This suggests not a lack of insight on the part of the actors but rather a premature, over-literal and forced interpretation on the part of the director. One will need to return to the abstract until the work emerges more concretely, and then back into the abstract, and then again back into the concrete. Little by little the group will reach a series of collective, if literally 'unspoken', agreements. Eventually, and even with very abstract pieces devised in an open-ended manner from blank starting points, the group will begin to reach a consensus.

When a piece feels 'solid' enough and has enough integrity to justify itself as a work of theatre, it can be presented in a public arena. Like a painting or novel, it must be complete and coherent – but no artist can ever guarantee the way a work will be perceived and a piece that is too 'obvious' or one-dimensional is liable to be poor work indeed. The artist must balance respect for the audience with respect for the work as a creative entity, and it may be that the interpretation of the artist, in this case the actors, and that of the audience will differ. Part of being a professional artist is the ability to let go of a work and to acknowledge the audience's right to interpret it in their own way. This of course places a heavy responsibility on the director.

Actors with learning disabilities may not fully comprehend (at least not conceptually) the way the final piece is read; they may not even comprehend the way in which a single action can be read differently if delivered in a subtly different manner. A touch on the face, for example, 'means' one thing if, at the same time, the actor looks intently into the other's eyes; it means something quite different if the same actor does not make eye contact. Whilst the director (and audience) can clearly read the differing impact of these two gestures, an actor with a learning disability may not be able to verbalise or discuss this difference and it is therefore impossible to distinguish what level of comprehension they will have of such a subtlety. Nevertheless when an actor demonstrates an ability to perform the action with integrity and authenticity (and by now the director should have a fine eye for the latter) it would suggest that the difference *is* understood, even if this understanding is emotional, sensory and primarily intuitive.

Ultimately we need somehow to arrive at a finished 'script' (albeit one that is not text-based): a coherent journey or sequential narrative with a 'beginning, a middle and an end'. By slowly piecing together sections of improvisation a narrative, perhaps purely an emotional or sensory one, will have begun to emerge. The task is to take the abstract and translate it into a coherent structure without at the same time sacrificing its abstract quality.

Plot and Narrative

If plot is understood to be the sequence of events within a storyline, and narrative generally taken to refer to the ways in which these events are told, it is clear that narrative need not be strictly linear. On the whole, however, in conventional theatre (as well as mainstream film and literature) plot and narrative tend roughly to coincide in their adherence to chronological time and in their emphasis on 'actual' rather than emotional events. A plot might run 'man meets woman, woman leaves man; man and woman get back together' but how long each segment lasts, what the choices of viewpoint and emphasis are, and even in what order these events are told, are all narrative choices – *how* the story is not *what* the story is. Audiences are increasingly familiar with the use of flashbacks and other devices that run counter to a chronological linear narrative and we are capable of managing two timescales concurrently in our heads. We are, however, less used to following sequences and images that do not fit into any timescale whatsoever or whose 'meaning' remains opaque.

When threading together the images and sequences – and this is the art of intuitive juxtaposition, to which we will return – a narrative will be implicit. A conventional plot or storyline, on the other hand, may or may not emerge. It might seem curious to speak of narrative without plot. Yet a narrative has its own rhythm, which usually works to deliver a plot with a particular emphasis. Indeed it is commonly held that there are only so many plotlines in the world and that these are merely told and retold thousands of times and in different media. Within genre work, plots can be almost identical and are part of the definition of the genre in the first place, along with certain other standard tropes such as lighting, minimal or melodramatic dialogue, music and even typefaces used in publicity (e.g. the standard 'Playbill' font of the classic Western). Without the shifting art of narrative, we would have watched the same film and read the same story a thousand times over. Plot without narrative is in fact almost inconceivable – except perhaps within publishers' *précis*. Narrative without conventional plot, by contrast, is more feasible than we might at first suppose.

Imagine the rhythms, textures and emotional emphases of narrative, whilst stripping away the plot that the narrative is ordinarily seen to serve. Just as abstract paintings, such as those of Jackson Pollock, have rhythm without any underlying literal reference (in fact Pollock's tutor taught him to copy the rhythms of famous Old Master paintings whilst purposefully omitting their content), it is possible to make poetic and visual narratives in the absence of conventional stories or literal meaning. Despite the experimentation in devised theatre and performance art over the last thirty years, for the most part mainstream theatre remains predominantly conventional and plot-driven, as does most mainstream and genre film and fiction. In this respect the work we describe is in the vein of visual and postmodern performance, except that, first, we advocate this work primarily because it reflects the actors' worldviews and, second, the absence of logical analysis right the way through the process is inevitably taken to its extreme by virtue of the actors' lack of recourse to conceptual thought. We are never employing an abstract image in order to express a concept (e.g. abstractness itself, or chaos, or enigma, or ambiguity); instead the images have emerged bodily and emotionally and as such their very essence is ambiguous. Any conceptualisation is retrospective – again the process runs counter to conventional practice.

For us narrative is the means of translating the material that will become the 'world' of the play (rather than the plot of the play). In effect it forms the theatrical *mise-en-scene*, as well as a parallel world with its own internal 'logic'. We will have hardly begun to grasp the dynamics of this 'otherworld' as we enter this final stage of the process. Nor will the actors have been able to articulate or objectify what they have generated as a result of the various exercises and strategies. We are left with a series of images and emotional 'areas' – constellations of motifs and feelings – that engage the group but whose 'meaning' is not yet clear. Piecing these areas together will at first involve a certain level of openness, taking hunches at what might be common threads and themes. We might even begin to work with something as seemingly fundamental as shapes, groupings or numbers of performers that are interesting when placed side by side. Such groupings need no explanation because the sort of narrative we are discussing is primarily intuited rather than understood, primarily poetic – even musical – rather than prosaic.

Heddon and Milling have grouped together and explored the work of contemporary theatre groups devising in a similar vein. In their discussion of 'postmodern performance', a term that is useful but which also poses problems in relation to the particular work that we describe, they emphasise the way in which many visually oriented devising groups find it difficult to accurately pinpoint the nature of the dramaturgical process:

Chance or randomness are combined with some unquantifiable, yet persistent, sense of 'appropriateness'. Though the work does not exist and is unknown in advance of its making there is nevertheless an assumption that there is a work to be 'discovered' or 'recognised'.[4]

They are right to highlight the 'unquantifiable' nature of the editing process in visual, bodily and emotive work: one of the key aspects, however, and which they touch on, is the art of poetic or intuitive juxtaposition.

Poetic Juxtaposition

Most people are familiar with the notion that in music the gaps between the notes are as important as the notes themselves. The notes may be the raw material, without which we would have only silence, but it is in the gaps between them that rhythm is constituted. In most other art forms the 'material' itself is widely considered to be the most important aspect, with the gaps between scenes, chapters, sentences, colours and forms (e.g. in painting) largely taken for granted by readers and viewers. Yet these gaps, as well as the choice of how one 'block' of material is placed next to another – whether these are words, areas of paint or shots in a film – are what really constitute composition, of which narrative is one particular form. This is perhaps especially clear in poetry, where meaning and what we might call 'image-sense' rely heavily not only on the choice but on the exacting combination, and placing, of words. Certain filmmakers have also paid particular attention to the way in which meaning is produced through the placing of images side-by-side, with the work of the pioneering Soviet filmmakers of the early twentieth century such as Sergei Eisenstein and Djiga Vertov noted for their attention to the way scenes are spliced together, 'montaged' or juxtaposed via the editing process. Vertov's work, as in *Man with a Movie Camera* (1929), is almost musical in its attention to rhythm and to the juxtaposition of visually similar but actually disparate images. (The horizontal lines of a window blind, for example, might be echoed in the next frame in an image connected to it only through its featuring some form of horizontal lines.) Eisenstein, perhaps the master of filmic montage, has even been described as 'thinking in pictures'.[5]

Minimalist artists such as Donald Judd also worked with the spaces in between 'units' as much as with the units themselves. Indeed Judd's works of the 1960s and 1970s, comprised of evenly spaced metal blocks and boxes, can barely be understood without taking into account at the same time the spaces between the units. Whilst minimalist art was rigid in its mathematical precision, and was subverted by 'human error' in the work of the post-minimalists and indeed the theatrical work stemming from it (as in that of Theatre of Mistakes), the importance of gaps and spacing in the making of meaning is clearly revealed here. The same gaps, furthermore, are not confined to modern and contemporary art. Throughout art history – the French Impressionists and Pointillists, the Italian Macchiaioli, even the loose brushwork of Titian and, later, Gainsborough – artists place equal creative weight on the material brushstrokes and the gaps between them.

The work of the Soviet constructivists and that of the (largely) American minimalists is 'modernist' in its relationship between content and form. That is, the meaning derived is considered to be self-contained and inherently related to the form in which the meaning is embodied, with little or no reference to shifting contexts and differing spectators. By contrast, most visual theatre work currently being created is largely considered 'postmodern', emphasising the breakdown of coherent, universal meanings and singular worldviews. Clearly, in relation to learning disability, these are entirely appropriate as concerns. Nevertheless the montage strategies of early modern forms and the balance between absence and presence, 'units' and the gaps between them, are also useful as precedents for certain narrative strategies.

These brief references to art and film may be useful when thinking about experimental visual theatre because they all involve making 'narrative' or compositional choices that are primarily visual, abstract and rhythmic rather than logical or related to the forward progression of a clear plotline. Furthermore such juxtapositions will tend to rely on an ability to think visually, intuitively and poetically rather than logically. We have mentioned already the difficulty of pinning down this particular working method. We are not referring to the ability to construct straightforward metaphor when we speak of the poetic. The French theorist Julia Kristeva has underlined the difference between poetic language and that of prose through her distinction between 'the semiotic'⁶ and 'the Symbolic', with the semiotic being a fundamental rhythmic impulse or bodily drive that underpins and underlies the overlaid literal or pragmatic meaning of the Symbolic. For Kristeva the semiotic is ordinarily hidden in language beneath the Symbolic, whilst it is only in poetic language that the semiotic is able to reveal itself as a constitutive force in making meaning. Other theorists, too, have spoken of the intuitive and visual aspects of meaning-making – such as Walter Benjamin's work on dialectical images, for example.[7] Whilst it is beyond the scope of this book to fully address these complex theories, what is crucial is that they propose a parallel way of making meaning – not literal and Symbolic but, conversely (and more rarely in common usage), image-driven, poetic and dialectic.

We are certainly on the side of the semiotic or poetic here, and especially of the dialectical, in its sense of 'resolving the differences between two views'. This is precisely what we advocate in relation to the resolution or creative juxtaposition of potentially contrasting scenes. Yet in mainstream theatre – and even to this day – the gaps between scenes are, by contrast, often treated incidentally, with the curtain lowered, or lights dimmed, to hide actual scene changes, quite literally covering over the construction of the narrative. Occasionally overtly postmodern devices are employed, with scenes being changed in full view of the audience, perhaps in recognition of Brecht's notion of 'distanciation' in which the audience is momentarily made aware of the falsity of the theatrical encounter. More rare still are works in which the scene changes constitute a part of the narrative itself. Furthermore mainstream theatre by its nature does not require particular attention to the way the scenes are juxtaposed in the first place, simply because the sequence is already fixed within the script. The playwright will have done the work of composition already, and whilst this is always a significant process involving crucial choices, it is perhaps made easier for the playwright when a plot-driven play has a straightforward chronological and linear narrative.

Moving beyond the 'postmodern' or Brechtian approach to scene changes, instead of simply revealing the mechanisms of stage management to the audience these changes can actually form part of the narrative; they can be explored creatively in their own right. Here the gap between scenes might become a scene in itself. Played out in this way there will be no clear gap at all but instead a fluid shift from one scene to the next, a fluidity that echoes our entire creative stance. What is crucial is that each scene will need to work in its own right and yet in conjunction with those that precede and follow it. Again, this is not about 'working' in a chronological sense but in a poetic sense. It might be that a high-energy scene involving many actors is placed alongside a quieter solo piece, so that the narrative emerges through the difference in energies, rhythms and ambiences. One may also choose to explore how, practically, the first set of actors leaves the stage to make way for the solo performer and through this exploration a further dynamic of the narrative is discovered. The interaction of the two might even inform the emerging plot by exploring the attitude of the group toward the soloist and vice versa.

We are not, of course, the only theatre practitioners to be aware of the ways in which the gaps between scenes, or the juxtaposition of different emotional or visual 'textures', will illuminate the scenes themselves. Theatre by ensembles such as The Wooster Group, working in New York under the general direction of Liz LeCompte, and Goat Island, an established Chicago-based ensemble, has been variously described as utilising collage or montage techniques. Both collage and montage rely on bringing together disparate elements in such a way that conventional meaning is ruptured – just as the Surrealist collages of Max Ernst played on the notion of the dream work whilst the montages of John Heartfield were employed in the service of powerful political statements. The aims, however, vary. Those interested in this form often refer to their attempt to reflect the pace of contemporary life with its snatches of imagery and sensory media overload. For Heddon and Milling this work functions primarily within the postmodern rubric of undermining 'master narratives' through fragmentation and 'provisional and partial' meaning.[8]

For us the use of juxtaposition is not political – our work simply aims to reflect the direct sensory and emotional experience of the actor with a learning disability. This itself might, of course, be read as a political gesture. If our desire to allow actors to speak in their own theatrical voice is also a desire to break down a singular viewpoint and normative assumptions about the 'right' way to think then, in a sense, the work does fall under this banner. Yet perhaps asking whether such work constitutes 'postmodern performance' is the wrong question. More provocatively, we might ask why such work is not already discussed under its rubric. The answer might be that work by those with learning disabilities is too often approached through the label of 'learning disabled theatre', a stance which makes impossible any genuine critical engagement.

Returning to the material and its organisation, the democratic way in which the devising process has been carried out up to this point will by definition have produced poetic juxtapositions since the sporadic nature of disconnected ideas and images hinders unnecessarily linear thinking. By finding a way to knit scenes together without watering them down to fit a 'grand narrative' we might discover that the disconnection between scenes creates its own particular series of dynamics. (The director must, equally, avoid simply 'jamming' scenes together – by having a bit of music played over two disconnected scenes, for example, with little attention to what this music will 'do' to the material.) It is this dynamic that requires particular attention: if we can bring two disconnected elements together in such a way as to allow them to work side by side we can produce powerful and explosive theatre.

Liz LeCompte of The Wooster Group suggests that, 'anything can co-exist together ... without being absorbed and regurgitated. They [the scenes or elements] are separate, and they can stay separate and at the same time inform each other – within the same work.'[9] Chris Johnston refers to a game called 'The Bridge', in which, given a theme, each actor privately works out a short scene based upon it. He or she will then present this to another actor and vice versa. They then have to come up with a story in which both scenes are incorporated exactly as they are, no matter how divergent the individual elements might be. As Johnston emphasises, each element should not be 'corrupted', nor is the aim total coherence.[10] For Johnston this game is played in order to promote egalitarian relationships between the actors; for us it highlights the potential for disparate scenes to be laid side by side, often with surprising results. The group might even find that some sort of cause and effect occurs, whereby one sequence takes on a new meaning by being placed after rather than before another. Heddon and Milling speak of the fact that, for the companies they discuss, 'the structuring process also simply demands the trying out of combinations in order to consider how different components work together, in terms of visual and rhythmic variations and textures, what their combinations might variously signify.'[11] What is exciting and challenging about the work in which we are engaged in is that this juxtaposition of two or more differing 'scenes' or 'narratives' often happens naturally in the devising process, simply because the actors bring these to the process unwittingly.

Whilst it is essential to remain fluid – as ever, preciousness and rigidity are unhelpful to the creative process – and open to 'sampling' the material for as long as possible, these sorts of happy accidents are to be welcomed. There is nothing wrong with 'logical' narrative if it arises organically rather than being foisted uncomfortably upon the work. Indeed, ultimately, a loosely 'readable' narrative is what one strives for; the point is that it should not be forced. If there are moments that are more easily graspable by the audience then these should not be dismissed in the name of wilful abstraction. The key is to let the work emerge of its own accord. We are not insistent on subverting traditional meaning for its own sake. Whilst we aim for work in which the poetic impulse is allowed to emerge, a complete rejection of 'Symbolic' structure would be unhelpful, even indecipherable.

Creative Problem Solving and Collaboration

We have talked of happy accidents and fortuitous juxtapositions. Because theatre has a physical presence it has pragmatic demands that the poet does not have to consider: the tangible environment of the play. Instead of dismissing the infrastructure of theatre it should be regarded as an essential creative tool; the more mechanical elements of theatre should be allowed to have a poetic function and also to inform the work. Companies such as The People Show have long allowed the realities of stage management to creatively impact on their theatre:

> Structural decisions, then, are often pragmatic: slow sections are contrasted with chaotic sections; loud with quiet; vertical use of space with horizontal use; the expected with the surprise, or the known with mystery. The question of 'how' also results in other pragmatic decisions: 'how can we get this prop to this place?' Or 'How can Laura get to this part of the stage?'[12]

For example, in a work directed by one of the authors a large metal disc was required to be hung on hooks and hoisted up at the back of the stage to create an image of a moon for the closing scene.[13] In a conventional narrative the logical solution might have been to employ stage hands to discreetly come on in a blackout to rig the disk and hoist it up before it was magically revealed. Instead the set change was incorporated into the work as a slow ritual in which the actors had to negotiate between them a way of getting the disk in place. Solving the problem became part of the drama. The scene allowed an exploration of the actors' physicalities, their individual bodily styles and the ways in which they interacted both with the prop and other actors. It also informed the play as a whole, which explored the notion of collective action.

We should not overlook the ways in which practical necessities can generate poetic meaning, just as 'happy accidents', for painters, can often take a work in a completely new direction. In theatre this might be as simple as a casting problem: in the authors' collective work interpreting *Pinocchio*, we worked with the actors to devise puppet characters for the scene in which Pinocchio visits the puppet theatre. In doing so we overlooked the fact that the only actor left available to play the puppet master, Swallowfire, was the actor already cast as Pinocchio's father. Because this actor has a very particular physicality and stage presence we felt it would be asking too much of the audience to 'suspend their disbelief' if he was seen playing two different characters. However, we realised that if he was 'unseen' and instead presented as a shadow on the walls of the puppet tent, this would not only disguise the identity of the actor but also add to the characterisation of Swallowfire as a foreboding figure, quite literally larger than life. This characterisation, so essential to the end effect, was nevertheless the result of a creative solution to a pragmatic problem.

The contributions of collaborators can also allow for interesting or novel approaches to a developing work. It can be helpful in any case, in order to remain objective, to have others in the room with the director since their interpretation of the material will inevitably differ and in this way multiple perspectives are encouraged. A collaborator can help to shift the nature of a scene from interesting but abstract to meaningful and 'readable'. In another of our works it took a collaborator working alongside two actors to shape what was initially an intriguing but 'unreadable' movement piece into a passionate love dance.[14] Whilst the actors were not able (or perhaps not prepared) to verbally articulate the romantic/sexual element of the newly shaped encounter, the authenticity of the final scene suggested a strong understanding of its meaning, even if this understanding was visceral and intuitive – intimacy, after all, is a feeling before it is a concept. The transformation of this piece, in relation to pragmatic demands, also enabled a development of the overall narrative, which was newly illuminated by the interpretation. If the characters are in love and the male character leaves at the end of the dance – because, for practical reasons, he is not involved in the next scene – this might then suggest that his feelings are too overpowering. Suddenly a necessary stage exit becomes a lovers' parting.

Design input can also be a stimulus for making sense of raw material and can often stem directly from early work with objects or props. In the same play that involved the love dance discussed above, the constituent elements of the work were arrived at through free improvisations: a suitcase full of clothes had led to a humorous dressing up routine, whilst an umbrella had instigated some interesting abstract movement work. Beginning to thread the various improvisation elements together it became clear that the 'dressing up' clothes needed to be present on stage. The designer's solution was to propose that they be hung on a washing line. Immediately this decision informed the other components of the work, with the umbrella taking on a greater significance in the 'chain of associations': washing–drying–wet–umbrella-rain. So, rather than starting with the clothes already on the line, it became a case of exploring: how might we hang the clothes up in the first place? Perhaps, in order to make sense of the umbrella routine, the washing is hung up once the rain has stopped. Here a narrative begins to emerge almost of its own accord. Further questions develop the narrative: why would five actors be hanging out washing together? What role might each take? Perhaps they all live in the same house together ... perhaps they only have one set of clothes each. The more robust the questioning the more bizarre the scenario – and bizarre scenarios can make for stronger narratives. Mark Long of The People Show, speaking in 1974 on a work in progress, describes the following situation:

> Derek has this idea for Edwardian boating. I have this idea for a Charlie Chan private detective who takes a shower every two minutes in the show. Jose has this idea of a man who's trying to pull down the Chinese wall and finds Rome behind it and gets attacked by a snake and a monster. Now that sounds bizarre, but there is actually ground on which those three ideas will go together.[15]

Visual theatre allows for such surreal tableaux to emerge – and to emerge with their own internal logic. The process becomes a balancing act between providing a logical framework and presenting abstract images within that framework.

For us the ideas are drawn out of the process and never 'brought into' the room in advance of the work. Either way, the temptation is to make the work 'comfortable', to smooth down the rough edges until the sense is entirely logical. This limits interpretative possibilities. The blurred line between fact and fantasy is what we seek to retain, and this also extends from the status of the 'reality' of the world of the play to that of the characters who inhabit it.

We have talked throughout this book about the ambiguous status of character in relation to actors with learning disabilities. We want finally to return to this theme to see how this hybrid character–actor functions or 'signifies' in practice. When it comes to the merging of character and actor, the personality of each individual actor is obviously significant. As such we refer here to examples from our own work, simply because we know the personalities of these actors.

The Actor/Character on Stage

An actor is left alone centre stage. He has contributed little to the performance so far and seems surplus to requirements. A piano stool is brought on and he is encouraged to sit. Gradually, large strips of white muslin are brought on by the other performers and wound around the seated figure. Eventually, he is wrapped entirely from head to foot by the strips of cloth. He becomes a packaged abstract form, remaining motionless throughout the sequence. The audience is aware of his breathing, and the occasional grunt or sound of the actor clearing his throat. A photographic image is now projected onto the cloth. At first we cannot make out the image; suddenly we see a large eye covering the whole of one side of the actor's wrapped head. The projector clicks; the image changes. We are thrown by the juxtaposition of one scale of human form projected onto another. We then begin to adjust our focus, shifting between the scale of the human form and that of the projected images. At last the cloth is slowly unwrapped. The images become clearer as the full extent of each photograph is displayed. They continue to change, forming a series. Portraits of children. Classic shots from family albums. A seaside figure in swimming trunks holding a bucket and spade. A tubby girl with bunches, posing for the camera in a photographer's studio. Some of these children clearly have Down

Syndrome. We begin to recognise similarities with the individuals performing in the play, connecting these images of childhood with some of the adult performers. One by one the strips of cloth are placed on the floor. The images no longer have a surface on which to be projected. They evaporate. The man walks off. From one side of the stage to the other, the actors walk along the cloths as if it were a pathway.

Here we have a double conflation of actor and character. The protagonist – or rather 'anti-protagonist' in his studied passivity – is, in reality, a quiet man who frequently sits and does very little. He is nevertheless a contributor in his own particular way and in improvisation work had allowed the actors to begin to wrap him up – a trusting and deeply authentic act undertaken quite consciously by the actor. As we have said, all offerings are valid even if they might seem to be negative or passive. Nor do we assume that such offerings are not capable of becoming powerful theatre. The trust of the actor in this instance is of paramount importance and this is clearly communicated to the audience: their response to this act may even be one of concern for the well-being of the individual. Will the actor respond? Stand up? Fight back? Throw off the cloths? Or will he allow himself to remain covered and, quite literally, be projected onto? It is often those people in life who say very little and who keep to themselves who find themselves the brunt of other people's psychological projections; the scene becomes a visual metaphor, yet one that emerged quite naturally through improvisation.

The non-verbal nature of this scene is particularly strong, especially since the scene comes towards the end of a work in which the audience may be intrigued to see whether this actor is going to 'do' something. The technical element of the photographic projections did not emerge through improvisation and so could be deemed an 'imposition'. The theme of childhood was, however, constructed through the work and inspired by the actors. A further aspect of this merging of actor and character is the slow realisation on the part of the audience that the images are of the actors themselves. This blurs the line between actuality and performance. Clearly, the actors were not 'acting' as children – and childhood is a stage in our life in which the need to 'act appropriately' and in relation to the demands of the world is not yet a burden. Since the actors as children are not performers, the status of the adult actors' presence on stage is also thrown into question. If they weren't acting then, are they acting now? Are they acting on stage? Are they acting in real life? And are they acting in life in relation to the projections of others? This is not autobiographical but universal – we have all been children. We have all, also, lost our innocence. Are we then all acting? What of our own authenticity?

Translation and Adaptation

So much of the work we have described and discussed in this book has revolved around the organic and authentic emergence of themes, motifs, 'stories' and images from the actors' personal experiences. It is possible – and sometimes desirable – to create work based on pre-existing stories. The challenge here is to work in such a way that the themes and characters of the story are relevant to the experiences of the actors, otherwise the exercise becomes a meaningless imposition. Clearly, we are not suggesting throwing aside all the approaches outlined previously and discarding the legacy of devised theatre in favour of a return to traditional script-led models. Indeed, as we have discussed, this would be impossible with actors who are unable to work authentically in this way.

Nevertheless the experimental processes utilised by many visual theatre and performance ensembles can also be employed in the service of a pre-existing story, as long as the use of this story remains an *adapted*, *translated* and *experimental* usage. Many devised theatre groups have referenced or drawn on existing stories and genres – creating a film noir-ish atmosphere, for example, without necessarily creating an actual spy-story. Others have openly referenced canonical works in a form of self-reflexive and subversive postmodern 'play' on the original material. Such work has merit but it comes from a rational place in which 'subversion' or inter-textuality are concepts in their own right. Like postmodern work generally, this approach also demands a level of knowledge of precisely the forms it is seeking to subvert or deconstruct.

For us the use of an existing story is only interesting when its themes can be drawn out at the service of the actors and are meaningful in their own right. It may be useful too in bridging the gap between what the audience expects and what the performer can provide, by giving the audience a pre-existing framework from which to come at a possibly abstract interpretation. Ultimately, existing stories are only worth telling if they mean something to the audience and, by the same token, to the actors. Because the themes in a strong story will resonate with people regardless of whether they know or comprehend the minutiae of the plot, with actors with learning disabilities it can be possible to lay an existing story or character onto a piece of work that has emerged in an improvisation. If, for example, an actor expresses anger at another actor because she will not give him the attention he wants, the director might choose to relate this universal theme to the story of King Lear and his anger toward his daughter Cordelia. It might seem extreme to propose the use of Shakespeare – of all playwrights – for work with actors who can struggle to communicate using everyday language, let alone sixteenth-century poetic language. Yet Shakespeare can work precisely because at the heart of his seemingly complex language are profound and universal emotions – anger, jealously, love, power-plays and so on – which have resonated with audiences for centuries.

This is not about providing access to Shakespeare because Shakespeare 'ought' to be known by everybody. It is because in Shakespeare's *words* are embedded profound *emotions* (and this is perhaps why, in a really strong and authentic performance of Shakespeare, audiences are often able to follow the emotional plot even if they do not fully understand all the words). In any case the actors will help determine what is truly relevant in any given story. A concept or theme that is too complex or which doesn't 'ring true' will simply not work and will therefore have to be discarded. The key is to remain clear about the motivation for the work. Is it to shoehorn performers with a different worldview into tried and tested models? Or is it to utilise their difference in the creation of something refreshing and new?

This is where actors with learning disabilities provide a genuine reminder to all theatre practitioners and indeed theatre-goers of the relevance of theatre. If a play no longer has the power to move us – or if it is performed endlessly in unoriginal, inauthentic and derivative ways (Brook's 'deadly theatre') – then, surely, it is not worth performing, regardless of the work's repute. Actors with learning disabilities invite us to cast off wear-worn devices and get back to the living heart of theatre.

10. Jon Tipton in Fallen Angels by The Shysters. © 2001 Michael E. Hall.

VII

Performance, Professionalism and the Public

If theatre is primarily a form of expressive communication, then it cannot truly exist in the absence of an audience. One always communicates *to* someone, whether an individual, a small group or a large paying public. The act of performance is also therefore an integral part of the development of an actor; in fact, until he or she has performed in public, the word 'actor' remains hypothetical to an extent. This is not the *only* work of the actor, of course, though the significant preparation, rehearsal and, in this case, devising processes, remain hidden from, and often forgotten by, the spectator. Yet unless an actor is exposed to an audience, to the potential for criticism as well as applause, the journey remains incomplete.

This book describes the stages through which a new ensemble of actors must pass, from entering the studio to entering the public arena, from being 'students' of theatre to professional practitioners. And we feel it is important to reiterate this emphasis on the notion of the 'professional'. Since the drama schools and universities make little provision for student or aspiring actors with learning disabilities, as we have noted before and will finally consider in our Conclusion, the work of 'training' must be undertaken by the director, albeit that the methods we advocate are far from didactic. Classical theatre training is precisely vocational, that is, it is intended to produce *professional* actors. This will be incorporated into their studies, from vocal projection training to 'practice' performances, as well as more mundane matters such as how to find an agent and how to handle first-night nerves. Again, we do not see why actors with learning disabilities should be short-changed in their training, and a director wishing to work with these actors will therefore need to be able to 'teach' certain aspects of professional practice, or rather, since we do not employ teaching methods as such, to enable the actors to learn them.

We raise this point because professional actors with learning disabilities will come up against a number of prejudices in their interactions with the wider public, and we need to be aware of these in order to be in a position to combat them. This should not have to be discussed; nor should other historically marginalised groups have had to fight for professional status in various fields – and indeed once a certain position has been attained labels tend to drop away. It is considered by many to be offensive now to speak of 'black writers' or 'women artists' – and especially, in the latter case, to have dedicated prizes and bookshelves for them. (We still find 'gay interest' sections in bookshops, as if gay people were only interested in 'gayness'; nevertheless they remain a useful resource for those who do, indeed, want access to more and better representations of gay people and their lives in a climate in which these are still rare.) Such groupings were enormously important in the early days of the equality movements, allowing 'black writing', for example, to be more widely available and easier to find, or redressing the absence of writings on female artists in the canon. They are now if not redundant then problematic, since they may be perceived as continuing the 'ghettoisation' they set out to redress; they have therefore outlived their usefulness. Likewise, we should not have to talk about the professionalism of professional actors simply because they have learning disabilities. Prevailing notions about learning disability and theatre, however, compel us to address the issue.

In fact we are at a curiously transitional point when it comes to theatre made by actors with learning disabilities. The label 'learning disability theatre' entered the theatrical language in the mid-1990s as a result of the proliferation of groups and companies of people with learning disabilities who were either using drama or making theatre as a means of self-expression. At the time there was a collective sense that these groups had something in common. Primarily this was the fact that many people with learning disabilities demonstrated an innate desire and a unique ability to express themselves through the performing arts. As with most emerging practices there was also a sense of isolation amongst practitioners and a feeling of collective strength gained by gathering under a single banner. However, as the practice has evolved it has become clear that there are many different approaches and, more significantly, many different motivations for engaging in the performing arts. For some the sole purpose is personal development and even the element of performance serves as a celebration of the achievement of the individual. For others the emphasis is much more clearly on the end product and employing the skills of the individual to serve a new theatre aesthetic. For others yet it is the political motivation of theatre made by people with learning disabilities to highlight issues about learning disability. All are equally valid. Yet in our view the use of the collective banner has contributed to a number of problems and is perhaps now redundant.

Theatre made by those with learning disabilities *about* learning disability tends at least to make some sense of this banner, since it then appears to refer to the subject of the work rather than the practitioners involved in it. (Taking this notion to its logical conclusion produces absurdities, however: should theatre dealing with the subject of war be referred to as 'war theatre'? That dealing with romance, 'romance theatre'? This absurdity surely highlights the problematic nature of the term.) Whilst it serves at least to draw attention to important advocacy work, the notion of 'learning disability theatre' also tends to lend credence to the misperception that this is the only subject about which actors with learning disabilities can make theatre.

This is exacerbated on two counts. The important work done by drama therapists and community theatre workers with people with learning disabilities has consistently emphasised process over product and purposely de-emphasised notions of skill, discernment, product, ambition and talent. This is rightly so, for the intended outcomes of such work are quite different. On the downside, however, the prevalence of drama therapy and relative absence of professional theatre work by actors with learning disabilities have meant that the public perception of the latter is distorted under the higher public visibility of the former. Second, because the theatrical vision of actors with learning disabilities is visual, poetic and experimental, it potentially invites criticism for its lack of observance of mainstream theatre skills such as vocal projection or physical technique. Those audiences most likely to understand and enjoy such work are likely to be those interested in experimental theatre generally; these, however, may be put off by the 'fact' of learning disability, precisely because of common misperceptions and the prevalence of the 'learning disability theatre' model. The situation, therefore, remains something of a vicious circle.

Learning Professional Practice

For those wishing to pursue theatre in its broadest professional context a professional theatre practice must be 'taught' just as it is taught in drama schools, even if the way it is taught will differ: we advocate turning the didactic model on its head and instead enabling the actors to *learn* through supported practice. First, however, it is useful to understand precisely what is meant by professionalism. Again, this may sound obvious, yet too few people, especially those new to a field, are aware that professionalism is not just a label delineating certain external conditions – paying audiences, nightly performances and so forth. Primarily, professionalism is an attitude, a stance, as well as a psychological ability to deal with the less exciting, or even potentially upsetting, aspects of any given field of work or creative endeavour. All students, in all vocations, as well as talented amateurs who move on to work professionally, will discover the moment in their training or career at which they begin to see themselves as 'professional'. For many, this moment can come as something of a shock.

The professional is defined as 'displaying a high level of competence or skill' and professional work as that which is 'undertaken or performed by people who are paid'. To begin to look closely at what makes a professional actor is to enter into complex and sensitive territory since it must by definition distance itself from amateur theatre. The distinction between the 'professional' and the 'amateur' in any field need not raise one term above the other, especially if we focus on the second part of the definition. Someone who is paid to do a job presumably has a level of competence in that area, yet we have all come across those who are happy to take payment for their work whilst remaining thoroughly unprofessional. Equally, someone who is exceptionally skilled or at least has that potential may choose actively not to practice professionally, preferring to retain a day job and a certain measure of freedom that goes with not having to worry about market needs.

Nevertheless the word 'amateur' does have negative connotations for many. We therefore enter difficult territory for two reasons. First, we would not wish to suggest that there is no point to an activity unless it is undertaken professionally: no point to sport unless one is striving to compete at the highest level; no point to creative writing unless one is seeking a publishing deal; no point to singing unless one has a contract with a recording agent; and, crucially, no point to drama unless one can attract a paying audience. All creative undertakings have the potential to be both pleasurable and beneficial. Nor does it go without saying that amateurs are always, or necessarily, unskilled. However, the professional does have to develop certain skills and even tolerances that the amateur does not. What fundamentally separates the amateur from the professional – and which contains no judgment about the superiority of either – is that the professional's work will be exposed to critical frameworks; they will also be exposed to the less-than-glamorous aspects of the job.

The shock of professionalism has been witnessed time and again by teachers, lecturers, managers – in short, anyone whose task it is to help develop another person's vocation or career. The fact that, especially within the arts, there are more graduates than practitioners in any given field is also testament to the nature of professionalism and to the fact that only a portion of those who enter the academies are fully aware of this when they begin. There is, for example, the element of boredom or pragmatism that comes with professional status. Amateur musicians and actors are often incredulous at claims that touring might ever become tedious or exhausting. Architecture students, meanwhile, dream of spaces rather than breezeblock and building regulations; this, alongside the very long training period, results in a vastly higher number of architecture students than practising architects. Art schools, too, are producing thousands of trained artists: few of them will make a living, even with funding available for experimental projects. Partly this reflects the exclusive and often highly subjective nature of the art world, but it also has to do with a critical faculty that must be developed by professional artists and which many students are unable to tolerate: the invitation to criticism that comes with public display.

The recognition of the difference between performing for fun and performing as a nightly obligation to audiences is therefore a significant aspect of the professional stance. This can be doubly surprising to the actor with a learning disability quite simply because, aside from the potential tedium, most have been told by society, directly or indirectly and from an early age, that they are 'disabled' from or 'incapable' of holding down a job or contributing in the wider social arena. This is the case even if their family has at least encouraged them to contribute within the domestic arena. Whilst the encroaching realisation that a performance *must* be entailed regardless of mood can be at first unwelcome, proving to themselves and others that they *can* work and *can* contribute can also be an exciting revelation to the actor.

For us the crucial differences between the professional and amateur stance are the levels of commitment to, engagement with and responsibility towards the audience. Is the actor making work in order to express themselves 'out loud' or do they wish to fully communicate with an audience? The highly skilled actor or artist who nevertheless refuses to engage with the differing perceptions of their potential viewers is not, in our view, fully professional. This is not about pandering or 'selling out', and the work we promote sets out in part to challenge audiences to accept, first, that an actor with a learning disability is entitled to, and able to, practise theatre and, second, that the audience might need to change their expectations about theatre (a stance that amateur theatre rarely takes). Nevertheless, we must respect the need for effectiveness of communication between one group of people and another. This is especially important in difficult or experimental work and it is for this reason that we discussed in the last chapter the need for the director to be aware of the work's 'readability'.

It is right that the development of professionalism should also be a development of the actor as a person; indeed when seeking authenticity it would be difficult to have one without the other. Performance is in many ways the natural culmination of a personal development process, and is intricately linked to the importance of release, expression and communication, which we have emphasised throughout this book. Even in therapeutic drama and other primarily private creative acts, performing or sharing the work (in small group performances or private writer's groups and so on) is felt by most as integral to the person's development, although of course there do exist people who are content to go through life never having revealed their work to others. Nevertheless, crucially, the professional and the amateur have very different audiences to contend with, with audiences for the former more inclined to judgment, sometimes critical or even harsh. These are also, we must note, 'paying audiences', and money is always symbolic of a particular sort of transaction. Having chosen to part with it, the spectator expects something in return, unlike the non-paying audience who may either perceive themselves as doing a favour or alternatively perceive the performance as a gift and therefore be duly grateful (and consequently, uncritical). Payment pushes the spectator into a more objective position, just as there is a very different power balance between a client and someone who is paid for a professional consultation or task, and that between the same person and his or her friends, who may be more positive about an issue but also less objective and therefore more prone to bias or vested interest. Bearing in mind this difference then, the perceptions of the audience are crucial; it is also crucial to fully prepare the actor and to aid him or her in becoming professional.

In line with this we must return to the point raised at the beginning of Chapter III as regards the aptitude for professional theatre work. Not all potential or aspiring actors will necessarily be able to go on to work as professional actors and the director has a duty – to the other actors in the ensemble, to the ensemble as a whole, to its work and indeed to its audiences – to accept when this is the case, regardless of how difficult this may be. This is also why the relationship between the director (as a person without learning disabilities) and the actors is so important: whilst this may be a contentious point, we are still a long way from seeing a situation whereby a person with a learning disability is able to provide a sustained and effective training programme for another person with a learning disability who wants to become an actor. Especially in a climate in which those with learning disabilities are often patronised by excessive praise for work that in fact has the potential for improvement, and they are therefore unwittingly discouraged from pursuing that improvement, the director's insistence on discernment remains crucial. This would remain the case if the director also had a learning disability.

The act of performance has an enormous impact on the culture of the ensemble. We have emphasised the importance of a performer's ability (and indeed desire) to work as part of a team – to support others and to respond to what they bring to the creative process. This is never more important than at the performance stage. Like any team activity, no amount of rehearsal or practise quite prepares one for the pressures of performance, during which the spotlight is quite literally upon you. Most people, quite naturally, panic under performance conditions. In the glare of the floodlights, or the scrutiny of the audience, the ensemble must be strong enough to be able to pull together in the face of the impulse to revert to an attitude of 'every man for himself'. The director must also be fully available to support the actors both as individuals and group members. In seeing the performance as a mere by-product or after-product of the creative process, we often assume that the director's job is complete after the dress rehearsal. This is not the case – the director must also oversee the learning phase of performance, supporting the actors and the show as they develop. Any committed director will in any case undertake to oversee and even develop the show throughout the entire run of its repeated performances.

Many of the methods and techniques described in this book are about developing the group and encouraging a collective sense of ownership. Basic techniques such as eye contact and the 'ritual' aspects of the warm-up and other exercises can engender a strong sense of the group that renders performance an extension of the daily work. If this is properly done then opening night becomes a celebration of the work that has been created together. Here the audience are invited witnesses. The sense of performing an important ritual, rather than being judged on the basis of a public spectacle, can also reduce the tendency to split off from or forget the group within the performance scenario.

Stage fright, nerves, panic attacks. All actors will have these to some degree and some may experience them quite severely. The veteran Donald Sutherland, for example, has confessed that he is, without fail, physically sick before going on stage. The outward manifestations of stage fright may lie at this more severe end for some actors with learning disabilities, who can become extremely agitated before early performances. (In other cases, however, nerves can be entirely absent, with the actor seemingly oblivious to the impending event, perhaps due to an absence of a clear concept of future experience, or alternatively an extreme openness and acceptance of experience.) Because an actor with a learning disability may not be able to conceptualise or name such manifestations as 'stage fright', the effects can be more intensely felt. Indeed, a recent experiment in which people were shown images of angry faces revealed that emotional responses were less intense when accompanied by captions.[1] Language, it seems, reduces the impact of overwhelming emotional experience. We have discussed the positive aspects of an absence of recourse to words in relation to heightened authenticity (if words can reduce emotional responses then they are also liable to hinder authentic responses). The negative side of this is that without recourse to the concept of 'stage fright', actors will have a harder job distancing themselves from or containing the emotion before going on stage. They may initially need support in making sense of what is happening to them mentally and physically and the director should be vigilant and prepared to deal with it. In our experience this 'unnameable feeling' tends in any case to be worked through in the course of repeated performance.

Performers also need to learn how to engage an audience whilst remaining firmly within the world of the performance. A crucial performance skill is the ability to maintain a 'straight face' regardless of audience response or, conversely, in more open, interactive types of performance such as comedy, to know when banter is getting out of hand or when a spontaneous routine is becoming dull. The situation is complicated for the work we describe since it is experimental in nature and in some cases more open-ended (e.g. where an actor works within parameters but where, within those parameters, the work is left open). This is the case for all forms in which there is a certain leeway as to what the actor might do, rather than each line and gesture being rigorously choreographed. To an extent the ability to read audience response is inherent to all good theatre, even when it is traditional.

The ability to come to the rescue when something goes wrong (when an accident occurs or somebody else forgets their lines) and save face on behalf of a play is also considered a crucial skill for the professional actor. The People Show speak of the way in which one member, Mike Figgis, was able to incorporate an accident (a bucket that was kicked accidentally) within a work. Experimental performance tends to allow for chance happenings and a certain element of improvisation. Unlike stand-up comedy, however, the direct address to or banter with an audience is not usually the main element of the work and the limits of the play's own 'universe' will need to be maintained. This balance between boundaries and limits and spontaneity and chance requires great skill on the part of both actor and director. For actors, it is essential to intuit the subtleties of audience response; for the director it is essential to make clear the limits within which this spontaneity occurs. Trust is also crucial. The group must be comfortable in the knowledge that any spontaneity must occur for the benefit of the play and not because one actor wishes to turn the spotlight more overtly upon him or herself: actors everywhere will know how subtly undermining it can be to have a scene surreptitiously 'stolen' in full view of an audience.

Having explicitly pursued authenticity, spontaneity and intuitive responses within the studio, the director must also ensure that these are contained within nightly performance. Charismatic and authentic performers must tread a fine line between crowd-pleasing and professionalism. Spontaneity can be spectacular but also distracting and unprofessional when, for example, it results in displays of ego. We see this with all sorts of public figures from sports stars to artists to singers. John McEnroe's charismatic displays of emotion eventually became tedious. When the artist Tracey Emin walked out of a discussion panel on live television, it was, for some, refreshing; for others it undermined the artist's credibility. Perhaps art celebrities and rock stars get away with extreme spontaneity more easily than others since a certain level of 'wildness' is expected, even demanded. Yet even here there comes a point where uncontrolled and haphazard appearances begin to be rejected by paying audiences.

We are not suggesting that actors with learning disabilities are prone to wild displays of ego, simply that the free expression encouraged through the devising process and sometimes open-ended scene playing, combined with a particular aptitude for authenticity, needs to be balanced with clear parameters. Some performers inherently understand the way in which the audience is both 'there and not there', that to respond too visibly to the audience is to break the spell of the piece (unless actor/audience interaction is part of the agreed playing style). Others at first do not, just as novice actors are not always aware of the way in which 'stealing a scene' can undermine a play as a whole. For all actors, and especially the more spontaneous, the ability to control one's ego and responses – even as the audience may lavish you with praise – is an essential skill. The director can play a fundamental role in supporting the actor to develop this skill through a continual process of feedback and analysis of each performance. It is essential to engender an ethos of learning within the company so that daily feedback and notes are not misconstrued as negative. If handled sensitively and in a supportive way, the learning that takes place in the course of a run can be the most valuable of all. After all, this is what all the work has been leading up to. It would be a wasted opportunity not to gain as much from the experience as possible and, given the costs and resources required in mounting a production, the individual must appreciate that these are precious opportunities for learning.

A failure to disguise a natural response to positive audience reactions can result in actors being visibly buoyed up by applause; it can be charming, even magnetic, but ultimately it is distracting and unsatisfying if an actor openly concurs with the audience's opinion that they are good or funny or charismatic. Rather like the comedian who fails to conceal his or her own amusement at a particular funny joke, or is unable to play 'deadpan' when required for a pun's effectiveness, such visible responses can appear smug or simply distracting. Equally, performances can be undermined when a performer is visibly ruffled by an error or poor audience response. Performers in all arenas – from sportspeople to actors – need to learn that the 'show must go on'. This is a doubly skilful task when the director is simultaneously encouraging extreme authenticity, and when the experimental nature of the performance allows a certain measure of improvisation. Again, like comedy, it may be tempting for an actor and initially very satisfying for an audience if, for example, a movement or word (or in comedy a catchphrase) is repeated because of a positive audience response. In Japanese Kabuki theatre this is accepted and positively encouraged: the performer makes a dramatic entrance, the audience shows their appreciation, the performer goes off and repeats the entrance. The comedian too will be constantly, if not consciously, measuring audience response – he will know that he can repeat a phrase or word that he had not intended to because it is working. Stand-up is a sort of jamming or constant semi-improvisation that allows for this, and there is also an element of improvised jamming in experimental theatre. Yet the performer must also intuit very quickly the exact point at which a move or phrase begins to lose its impact.

How are these complex skills learned? Quite simply, by mirroring conventional actor training – that is, building up to a level of professionalism through choosing performance contexts appropriate for the stage at which the actors have arrived in their professional development. Showing works-in-progress, in the initial stages, to invited but slightly more sympathetic audiences before exposing actors to the 'paying public' can be helpful in allowing actors to come to terms with audience expectation.[2] Performances to friends and contemporaries throughout the course of study are worth encouraging, as are performances to more critical and informed audiences of peer practitioners and suchlike who may have a keen interest in supporting the work.

Finally an actor, like all professional artists, will need to come to the understanding that an audience might – and probably will – interpret the work differently to the way in which the actor (or artist or writer) imagines it. The ensemble of actors who have so far retained total ownership of the work must also learn, like all artists, to detach from it. This can be particularly difficult, even disenchanting. Nevertheless through experience actors, artists, authors and other creative professionals learn to release their work into the wider world. This remains the case regardless of the presence or absence of learning disabilities – and perhaps after all this is the true measure of the professional. For many people, it remains the hardest part of creative activity and perhaps the most compelling reason for retaining amateur status. Having put themselves wholly, authentically and creatively into the work, the actors must also have the openness and willingness to let it go.

Audience Expectation and Response

Experimental work comes with its own difficulties. If one aspect of professionalism is the need to communicate with an audience, when this communication is made purposefully transparent we are reduced to the theatrical equivalent of low-grade 'genre' fiction. Even genre fiction (at least the best of it), which for the most part sticks within pre-formulated and easily understandable criteria, offers or communicates something new to its reader within each title. Experimental work lies at the other end of the spectrum, where an audience knows little about what they are about to see or read and has placed significant trust in the artist/actor/author. People go to the theatre for numerous reasons, just as they read fiction for numerous reasons, ranging from light entertainment or distraction to the desire to inhabit other-worlds, to feel new things, to have new experiences, to be shocked or moved or even changed in some way. With theatre and other live performance forms there is an additional factor: the desire for significant human interaction in the live and present moment.

By definition, experimental or avant-garde work pushes or challenges the boundaries of the current critical framework. How can it be measured when the very criteria for measurement are precisely what it sets out to challenge? Often the person making this work is already established as a professional in the first place, and then decides to test the boundaries of the form. The acceptance of experimentalism may also ironically rely on conventional training frameworks: a person who has officially graduated from an arts course is in effect 'peer reviewed' previous to embarking on criteria-altering work, and the best schools encourage this. It may be that many people begin at once to push against the conventional norms – as happened with devised theatre – and here the sheer force of numbers shifts the criteria. There may even be economic factors, since it is perhaps easier to go out on a limb when one's livelihood does not depend on it, and it is also easier to publicise and promote experimental work if one has recourse to the finances to buy advertising, rent venues, draw crowds and even, in the heyday of avant-gardism, print manifestos.

For actors with learning disabilities such opportunities are rare: many are caught up in the 'benefits system' whereby due to the lack of employment opportunities available most have to claim benefits, which are then retracted if part-time work is taken. Almost none are trained conventionally through the theatre education system and thus do not have the 'qualifying criteria' that can easily support experimental work. On the whole, the work of actors with learning disabilities has been shown and continues to be shown professionally only because they have had access to and opportunities to work with directors or other facilitators who are already part of the professional theatre system. Even here critical frameworks can be problematic due to 'ghettoisation' – as we have noted, theatre made by actors with learning disabilities is frequently conflated with the notion of 'learning disability theatre' and thus either ignored by wider audiences or read through inappropriate frameworks. We might wonder how many theatre-goers choose to see a performance involving actors with learning disabilities based on the criteria of enjoyment or interest alone, rather than out of the desire to support what they perceive as a 'worthy' enterprise; even after many years of development work in this area, perceptions are still blighted by such notions.

Two crucial areas need to be considered as regards audiences and in relation to the particular type of theatre made by actors with learning disabilities that forms the subject of this book. Both relate to audience expectation. First, too many people perceive those with learning disabilities as being by definition outside of 'mainstream society' and therefore mainstream social contribution – even when this 'mainstream' is, in reality, 'fringe' or experimental. This raises the question of how the fact of the actors' disabilities comes into play in a spectator's decision to go to see a work and what prejudices or notions they then bring with them. If the fact is mentioned in attendant publicity, this immediately 'earmarks' the work as 'learning disability theatre' and, also, subjugates the actors to a label. If it is not mentioned, there is the risk of audiences feeling they have not been given full information. The necessity and even ethical problematic of informing audiences in advance is debatable, except where the work is *about* learning disability. To return to early political devised theatre, would an ensemble comprised solely of gay actors be compelled to inform the audience of their sexuality if the work itself was not about gay issues? There is a difference, however, and one that makes this issue particularly sensitive. We have argued that whilst the subject matter itself may not be about 'disability issues', its very substance and imagery is directly informed by the particular attitudes and approaches precisely of those with learning disabilities. Therefore whilst *not* mentioning the fact might seem the more appropriate approach, in some ways it is akin to failing to signal – for example, not telling people that there is an all-gay cast when a play is not *about* being gay but its imagery stems directly from the actors' experiences of the world *as* gay people. In reality, the authors have used both approaches; both have their drawbacks and advantages and the debate as to which is the more appropriate remains complex.

Either way, audiences are liable to perceive a 'difference' in the actors even where that difference is not obviously visible (as it is with

Down Syndrome) and even where they are unable to pin this difference down.[3] A particular intensity, a unique movement style, a searing authenticity that they have not come across before – the difference is present; it is, in fact, part of what makes the work what it is. How does this then inform critical responses to the work? There is a danger that this 'unique' or 'different' quality is dismissed as 'a learning disability thing'. And, in a sense, it is. But this holds the risk of overlooking the technical work that the actors have done in honing and training their skills. Certain natural traits may *enhance* the work, just as any charismatic performer or 'natural' will bring this element of themselves fruitfully into their performance. This should not mean that the work is not critically perceived and appraised within professional criteria. In fact, it may even be that actors with learning disabilities have to work harder and produce even better quality work than other actors, in order to allow the theatre itself to break through certain presumptions or stereotypical attitudes, which can range from the positive yet patronising to outright dismissal. Again, this should not have to be the case (although of course all actors should strive to make the best work possible), just as it should not be the case that women or black people have historically had to work harder than men or white people in order to prove their worth. (This is a seemingly outdated attitude that nevertheless still holds true for many people.) In the current climate it does seem to be the case that the spotlight is more brutally focused on marginalised groups when it comes to cutting through prejudice and misperception.

Second, since the worldview and theatrical language of actors with learning disabilities is in so many respects quite different from that of traditional theatre, the work can only be fully understood and appraised through a critical framework that appropriately grasps the language of experimental theatre. Ironically, as we have noted in the Introduction to this book, experimental theatre work is now so well established that it has acquired its own body of literature. It is even so well recognised that young performance students have sometimes tended to copy its visual style without too much thought to the theatrical processes that have led to certain common visual characteristics. Certainly practitioners working within these forms must be careful not to parody themselves – this happens when authenticity is overlooked, and each new work should be approached on its own terms. With experimental theatre increasingly validated, at least amongst certain audiences and reviewers, it is peculiar then that such experimentalism in works involving actors with learning disabilities can be dismissed by audiences and critics. Perhaps because of a notion that experimental theatre is 'high concept', and also because of the 'learning disability theatre' banner, those audiences best placed to enter into these visual worlds are not always those most likely to go to see them. And what is perceived as 'normal' by audiences used to the visual/physical theatre circuit, for example, may be perceived as overly complex or confusing by audiences more used to conventional theatre.

There are ways of aiding audiences in understanding the poetic and visual nature of such work, and these directorial decisions must be carefully taken. These are also little different to the decisions that face any maker of visual or postmodern theatre, except that 'mainstream experimental theatre' (to coin a phrase) has at least acquired a dedicated fan base who have learned how to read such work and who therefore come prepared. For this reason audience confusion may not be quite such a concern for high-profile ensembles whose visual style is well established and widely known. Nevertheless it is always good practice for theatre-makers to strive to widen audiences, as long as they are able to do so without compromising the work that they are making. To refuse to engage with audience needs is potentially to become closed-minded and unable to discern between 'readable' experimentalism and purposeful obscurity. One should hold one's ground – refusing, for example, to produce a happy ending where the ensemble feels strongly that an unhappy ending is more appropriate – and resist the pressure to simplify or 'dumb down' the work to the point at which it loses its meaning. At the same time the decisions made about how best to weave the images and scenes together should bear in mind the need for some kind of readability from an audience perspective, even if this is far from the standard linear narratives of the mainstream style.

Publicity literature, programme notes and announcements incorporated as part of the work are other ways to prepare the audience for an abstract style, although one must be careful that such announcements are not employed to let the work's own readability 'off the hook'. In any case, what one person finds logical and readable another may find obscure and alienating, and we cannot hope to appeal to everyone. Working primarily with a visual language, one cannot expect – nor would we want – singular, obvious meanings to emerge. The point of 'poetic work' is to retain enough ambiguity to allow the image to resonate on a number of levels; at the same time ambiguity to the point of meaninglessness will inevitably be unsatisfying. The ability to see the point at which enigma becomes confusion is a skill that is almost impossible to teach; it must be grappled with and learned through practice.

Live performance does have one advantage in this respect over other forms such as literature and fine art – that is, since it is repeated nightly, it is open to potential change. A novel, once published, is fixed forever – if readers fail to 'get' the work there is little the writer can do except to swallow the bad reviews and try for better clarity next time. With live performance forms, which also only come fully alive under the gaze of an audience, there is the potential for further honing of the work, as long as this does not compromise the integrity of the work itself and as long as it does not become an exercise in pandering to the whims of audiences. Singers know this: famous songs can be updated or even completely reworked in later concerts; even on an album tour, the confident singer or band will change the particular emphasis in mood or singing style dependent on the context – and even on the singer's own mood on any particular night. Experimental theatre also holds the potential for subtle developments and shifts of tone, especially since it incorporates looser elements within a fixed framework. There are degrees of change – changing the emotional tone of an ending can be done in extreme cases but contains the risk of undermining the work's integrity, for instance. More usually, the material and its various levels of meaning might simply become clearer in the course of repetition, with material further 'unearthed' in the clear light of the audience's gaze and further connections discovered that, through small adjustments, can be subtly and organically incorporated into the work. In this way theatre is never wholly fixed and it is perhaps this fluidity that makes live performance such a satisfying form.

The routine of touring and performing, then, are essential to the 'professionalisation' of the actor and may even be essential to the progression of the work of theatre itself, although of course one will only put on in public work that, as far as the ensemble can possibly be aware, is complete in itself at the time. Far from abandoning the job of work at the dress rehearsal, or even after opening night, the director's role is ongoing, just as the actors' work is hardly complete until the piece of theatre that they have created is also performed. If at this stage the director stops short with his or her support, or the actors with their commitment, they will have done the work a disservice.

Discernment, rigour, dedication and the ability to be critical and objective are all professional traits. Perhaps apart from objectivity (since the work we describe encourages more than most subjective and authentic expression, and since such a stance is always harder to adopt from an internal rather than external viewpoint), all are as essential for the actor to acquire as they are for the director to uphold. We have raised the issue of professionalism in the face of general attitudes, built up over the last thirty years, that have regarded critical positions, discernment and ambition as limiting, elitist and potentially undermining of those less able to 'compete' within these frameworks. Postmodernism has also seen singular viewpoints and fixed critical positions abandoned: all viewpoints are equal and anything goes. Whilst this is, on the whole, a positive development, it has also led to an attitude in which sloppy work is ever more defensible. Either the audience has failed to understand it, having brought to it a different viewpoint, or, alternatively, it does not really matter because at least the person tried. Such a view is in fact quite widespread and pertains to all creative endeavours – hence the current difficulty in talking about such notions as 'good' and 'bad' artworks.

This attitude is even more prevalent when it comes to groups of people on behalf of whom others have made the decision that aspirations may not be achievable. Concerned not to expose those with learning disabilities to potential failure and instead to encourage self-esteem, an attitude that promotes process over product (the 'taking part' over 'the winning') has been prevalent. This is understandable but ultimately unhelpful. The danger is that those with learning disabilities simply feel more hopeless, since such a view tends to promote the notion that they will, inevitably, fail at their endeavours. Alternatively, as we have noted, this attitude can also give people a distorted sense of the level of their current achievement and abilities, discouraging them from applying themselves to more rigorous and ultimately more rewarding training processes. More problematically still, such a stance promotes the idea that people with learning disabilities are fundamentally and equivocally different from other people: not equipped to be judged by the same standards applied to others; not allowed, like other people, the right to succeed or even the right to fail. Such attitudes can ironically contribute to reducing rather than raising self-esteem. Essential to the success of the work under discussion is how the people making it regard it and the value that they themselves place upon it. The actors have chosen to make professional work and it should be judged, promoted and supported as such. After all, if the actors themselves are not encouraged to value their work or to take it seriously, how can we expect audiences to do the same?

11. Members of Full Body and the Voice Youth Theatre in a version of The Tempest. © 2007 Jo McFarlane.

Conclusion:
Questions for the Future

Actors with learning disabilities have been making, and continue to make, significant and complex theatrical work. Their presence on screen is also currently being felt and is even receiving a certain amount of interest in the media. This would seem to point both to a wider acknowledgement in society of the abilities of those with learning disabilities and a widened dramatic remit. Sadly, however, such work is both rare and relatively little known, and professional actors with learning disabilities – whether on stage or screen – are also few and far between, with the parts they are offered frequently restricted to roles in works *about* learning disability, rather than being perceived as characters in their own right. The work we discuss in this book is testament to the exciting developments in theatre produced by actors with learning disabilities outside of these limiting roles. The fact that this book is the first to discuss the work of actors with learning disabilities made on their own terms is, however, also reflective of their lack of general visibility.

Perhaps this simply reflects the current theatrical climate, in which script-led work driven by the playwright's vision – work both difficult for and of little interest to those who do not see the world through primarily verbal means – still attracts significantly larger audiences than its visual or physical counterparts. Despite the developments in theatre practice and 'languages' over the last thirty or so years, experimental ensembles still have a harder time than conventional companies in reaching audiences, though they do at least have the advantage of small but dedicated followings, audiences who are versed in the language of non-linear meaning and who know how to read such work. When theatre is non-mainstream in its form, and when the practitioners who make it are also quite wrongly perceived as being 'outside of the mainstream', the problems of access are twofold. In this latter respect the public visibility of such work also reflects the wider societal situation of people with learning disabilities.

We noted in the Introduction to this book the recent press focus on screen actors with learning disabilities, and also the current campaign, aimed at employers, which addresses the lack of employment opportunities for those with, in this case, Down Syndrome. These are small but significant steps towards a recognition of the vast misperceptions around learning disability, misperceptions that are even ingrained in 'medical' definitions of the term, which tend to emphasise 'lacks', 'failures' and 'impairments' rather than difference, individuality and differently oriented skills. People with learning disabilities are virtually the only marginalised group of people in our society who continue to be defined solely by what they are unable to do. The general public's understanding of learning disability, and even of the term's meaning, also remains hopelessly poor, with learning disability frequently conflated with mental illness, which is still widely stigmatised – in itself an archaic and unforgivable attitude at the beginning of the twenty-first century.

Yet these perceptions have hardly been helped by the ways in which disability and learning disability have been presented to the public by charities. The old image of the 'handicapped' child, epitomised by the mannequin collecting box that, with its callipers and sorrowful stance, stood outside shops until well into the 1970s, did little to encourage a positive view of disability, much less to promote notions of equality. This has since been replaced by the more sophisticated and well-intentioned representations of people with learning disabilities through such campaigns as 'Children in Need' as well as local media reportage. We cannot doubt that the money and awareness raised by such campaigns is useful. Yet this awareness remains deeply limited by the prevalence of the 'tragedy model' (recognised by the disability movement) and the de-humanising conflation of individual people into stereotypes or 'montages' of images that strip individuals of their subjectivity and instead present them as mere ciphers for a wider phenomenon: 'disabledness'. Tom Shakespeare has noted that:

> [one of] the tendencies of non-disabled society is to see all disabled people as the same. All people with Down Syndrome are like this, all people with restricted growth are like that, that's what blind people are like. So that the individual disappears and they become a type.[1]

The systematic way in which campaigns employ particular representational tropes through the use of editing and camerawork, depressingly serious voiceovers and heartstring-tugging music in order to elicit a combination of pity, patronisation and distancing (or 'othering') would require a chapter in itself to deconstruct. Suffice to say that, regardless of the financial benefits of such campaigns, nothing about them promotes respect or even equality for the people who 'we' (i.e. 'able people') are so briefly keen to help. Even media reportage, which is welcome if it increases visibility, can tend to replicate the tragedy model through its attempts to turn it on its head: such articles tend to revolve around a sense of amazement at the achievements of someone with a learning disability, as if such achievement were extraordinary or miraculous (and therefore, of course, newsworthy). So pervasive are such views that we find it hard to conceive of people with learning disabilities as being anything other than in need of our support. Especially because for many people with learning disabilities, their 'different' appearance or behaviour is visually evident, the attitude is even akin to a form of racism. Furthermore, as Tom Shakespeare also points out, 'One of the things that racists and bigots of all types do is deny their victims an emotional range, deny their feelings, make them into an object.'[2] By contrast with racism, however, such views are still upheld and promoted by those who are supposedly on their side.

In the face of such dubious representations, it is hardly surprising how often people look askance at the idea of someone with a learning disability making meaningful, professional creative work;

or even of holding down a job. They consolidate the belief that those with learning disabilities are, at least ordinarily, unable to contribute to society in any purposeful way. As we have noted previously, this is perhaps exacerbated by the fact that two of the skills affected by learning disability are writing and eloquent verbalisation, so that few have been able to speak out against such pervasive and pernicious stereotypes, in the way that people with physical impairments have been able to do. Yet people with learning disabilities can and do communicate: theatre is one such forum for communication.

Considerations for Training

The higher education system has not been forthcoming in its desire to facilitate such communication. Barred from conventional university theatre and performance departments, due to entry requirements based on qualifications as well as the academic nature of the teaching programmes, and barred too from vocational drama schools, because these actors do not fit easily within the traditional training model, the aspiring actor who has a learning disability has almost no access to appropriate training. The processes described in this book – though never officially intended as such – provide a forum, and there are others, though they are few and far between. It remains a matter of luck – a postcode lottery, in fact – as to whether a professionally based group or company happens to be working in the actor's vicinity. Much of what is described in this book in any case alludes to a form of actor training that is significantly different to that taught in drama schools. Colleges and universities, perhaps more attuned to the fact that students are looking for a more general appreciation of the performing arts and a broader range of employment prospects, do embrace some of the techniques outlined in this book. Universities have also begun to address the issue of learning disability in the Community Arts and Applied Theatre curricula, and many courses examine and promote the qualities of ensemble and devised work that will at least prepare some non-disabled practitioners for the kind of approaches we have outlined here. Nevertheless these curricula are aimed at those without learning disabilities; this conundrum, of course, also applies to this book, which is written by, and by definition intended to be read by, those without a learning disability.

Yet performance is, in essence, a physical and visual form and should hold fewer barriers for those with learning disabilities. One would therefore think that the drama schools and schools of performing arts might have a fruitful part to play. Sadly, these remain for the most part focused on equipping students to survive in a ruthlessly competitive industry. They may even feel that such an education would be 'wasted' on an actor who is unlikely, in the current climate, to gain regular employment. Furthermore the curricula as they stand would need to be significantly more flexible in order to incorporate the different models of learning that we advocate. Trying to force an inappropriate, inauthentic and even useless training model onto people who require quite a different sort of training altogether is, as we have noted, both difficult and ultimately futile. It would only result in 'wooden' actors with a set of largely mimicked and inappropriate skills; in short, people who can replicate the appearance of acting whilst the true art of drama is left at the stage door.

Flexible, varied or modular curricula might address this problem; they would also undoubtedly bring their own financial and functional concerns, and seen in this light it is understandable that the drama schools continue to struggle to embrace the issues fully. It is also, ultimately, unacceptable. Similar arguments were used for years to absolve employers from ensuring proper wheelchair access, for example, and continued discrimination is always bolstered, historically, by such financial and pragmatic arguments. Discrimination against those with learning disabilities will eventually have to be addressed, regardless of the cost. Perhaps only when actors with learning disabilities become more publicly visible and begin to get more work, as they are already doing in film, television and also on stage (Out of Joint, the New Vic, Stoke-on-Trent, and Theatre Centre are three such companies who have all recently hired an actor with a learning disability) will commercial forces galvanise the drama schools to respond. This increased availability of work for actors (as well as the wider availability of work for those with a learning disability) might also begin to dent the dynamic of the 'benefits trap'. Aside from its financial implications, this scenario can undermine the self-esteem of the actor who may never quite feel 'fully professional' until he or she is able to earn some sort of living from their work. It may even be that struggling with a day job, like other jobbing actors, would increase rather than decrease the self-esteem of actors with learning disabilities who wish, above all, to be treated like 'ordinary' people.

In the event of drama schools responding to this changing climate – a scenario we sincerely hope to see realised – the question will return to the ways in which such training is undertaken. Might such institutions have the courage to adapt their criteria to the particular talents of the students? There are encouraging signs, with actor Christopher Eccleston, for example, openly and positively speaking about learning to adapt his processes when working with the talents of Dorothy Cockin and Peter Kirby, both actors with learning disabilities, in the BBC drama *Flesh and Blood*. Is it possible to bridge the gap between mainstream, traditional disciplines and the organic, authenticity-oriented, actor-led training approaches proposed in this book? If so, who will train the actors? Who, indeed, will train the trainers? And which institutions will ultimately have the conviction to make the first move?

Institutions will have to deal with the problematic elements of the more 'exclusive' elements of current working practices. We would even argue that drama training as a whole would benefit from such an overhaul. One has to ask how many of the predominant customs and practices in mainstream theatre are still appropriate. Must text-based work still dominate to such an extent in the early twenty-first century? How necessary is it to continue to use industry jargon – stage right, stage left, 'green rooms', 'flyrails'? Are we aware of how confusing and excluding these terms can be? So much of current drama training still reeks of Brook's 'deadly theatre', its velvet-curtains and floodlights and pomp. Is it not time to inject some life back into its shell?

Marketing, Touring and Critical Frameworks

It is not only the drama schools who will need to re-evaluate their position, methods and frameworks if such work is to be encouraged and promoted. There are questions, too, about how it is critically received and evaluated. These factors, in turn, will weigh on the minds of anyone whose aim it is to promote such work. We touched in the final chapter of this book on issues around the marketing of theatre made by actors with learning disabilities, primarily, whether or not it is helpful or even appropriate to publicise this theatre with direct reference to the learning disabilities of the actors. There are also questions, unsurprisingly, about visibility. Invariably, the actors will not be 'recognised' names, nor, given that the work is likely to be devised, will it have been written by a recognised playwright. By the same token, because the work is new, the title of the piece will also be unfamiliar. There is, in so many ways, very little for a paying public to put their trust in and, as such, all but the most daring theatre-goers may choose to steer clear. The latter are concerns that all devised companies will share, particularly those without a long track-history or fan base. The 'learning disability' issue is merely one more challenging factor.

A number of companies at the vanguard of experimental work with actors with learning disabilities have therefore aimed to present work that recognisably fulfils at least one of the criteria described above. They might consciously employ a recognised writer or performer, who will bring a certain 'seal of approval' to the piece, or alternatively present an unusual version of an already well-known story or play. In doing so, the company will of course be confronted immediately with the next hurdle: whether, in the promotional literature, to mention the fact that the company is comprised of actors with learning disabilities or not. As we have said, this is a complex debate and is perhaps best decided in the context of the individual work.

What is imperative in all cases is that the work be presented in a professional, even highly respected, theatre setting. Too often such companies are offered 'second best' (when it comes to the choice of venue, for instance) and it is all too easy to accept such offers in the fear that nothing better may be available. This amounts to a form of lack of self-esteem on the part of theatre companies and can become a self-fulfilling prophecy. Historically, prejudicial values have shifted only when those involved have begun to refuse to accept the situation. The choice of composers, designers and technicians are important, too. High production values should be maintained at all costs; this will include working with the best practitioners as collaborators. The development of this work therefore requires the faith of a number of key people in the profession who are prepared to trust its worth and to lay their professional credentials on the line. They must also take credit for helping to bring the work into the public domain. One cannot underestimate, also, the impact of international visibility through touring. European funding has played a crucial role in enabling this to happen, with Heart and Soul being one of the first companies of performers with learning disabilities to tour in Europe, and our own companies have also benefited from these opportunities. From the point of view of 'patronage', the EU funding streams should not be overlooked. Touring internationally not only boosts the profile of theatre companies, it also significantly boosts the confidence of the ensemble.

Getting the work 'out there' is one matter. Its critical reception is another. We have talked about the way that audiences understand – or, sometimes, fail to understand – visual/physical theatre forms. Critics are presented with another conundrum. The work is unusual, different. It therefore needs to be assessed within unusual and experimental, rather than conventional, theatrical criteria. This means that commentators run the risk of being accused of patronisation, perhaps unreasonably, if they assess the work differently to that of a standard theatrical presentation, or, justifiably, if they begin, consciously or not, to make 'allowances' for the fact that the actors bring a different aesthetic to the performance. It is also difficult to make any kind of qualitative judgment about work with which there is so little to compare. As more actors with learning disabilities come to prominence, and as more work is produced in this vein, it is to be hoped that a new set of criteria will be established by which we will be more able to judge the quality and merits of the work. A new mindset cannot be imposed but, like the development of physical and devised theatre in the 1960s and 1970s, it has to evolve through exposure and eventual acceptance.

Thoughts on the Future

At the risk of self-redundancy, one would like to think that there would, one day, be little need for companies such as Full Body and the Voice, The Shysters and others who have trained their own actors as well as creating theatre. The new theatre groups might instead be able to cast trained actors for specific productions in the usual manner, though that does, admittedly, run the risk of losing the more interesting qualities of ensemble working. We might also expect that in the future actors with and without disabilities will increasingly work together, with each being informed and inspired by the other's different theatrical approaches.

Entrenched attitudes can take generations to change. We sense, however, that change is already under way. We are only just emerging from the 'rude to stare' mentality that has prevented people from acknowledging those with learning disabilities, let alone their work in the performance arena. The reality of the theatre work under discussion in this book requires quite an opposite stance, in fact: it is only by really looking at the individual that we are able to engage with him or her beyond the veil of prejudice. And it is only through true engagement that we are able to make, and enjoy, authentic theatre.

Notes

I Equality

1. Jane Campbell and Michael Oliver, *Disability Politics: Understanding our Past, Changing our Future*, Routledge, London and New York, 1996, p. 62.

2. See Tom Shakespeare, *Disability Rights and Wrongs*, Routledge, London and New York, 2006.

3. Ed Berman of Inter-Action is widely acknowledged as an early pioneer of work for people with learning disabilities and is credited with inspiring a number of theatre companies: Interplay Theatre, and Leeds and Action Space Mobile, to name just two. Jon Palmer's work in the 1990s as Artistic Director of Interplay further explored dynamic ways in which to engage audience members with profound and multiple learning disabilities.

4. Deirdre Heddon and Jane Milling, *Devising Performance: A Critical History*, Palgrave Macmillan, Basingstoke and New York, 2006, p. 100.

5. Interestingly, scientists such as Steven Pinker have recently begun to support this view. Pinker's thoughts on this subject are contained in many of his books – see in particular *The Language Instinct*, Harper Perennial Modern Classics, London, 2007.

6. This is in line with the work of French feminist thinkers such as Luce Irigaray, Julia Kristeva and Hélène Cixous, whose work has been collectively described as "l'écriture féminine' or 'writing the body'.

7. Heddon and Milling: *Devising Performance*, p. 116.

8. Ibid., p. 117.

9. Chris Johnston, *House of Games: Making Theatre from Everyday Life*, Nick Hern Books, London, 2005, p. x.

10. Ibid., p. xi.

11. Catherine Itzin, *British Alternative Theatre Directory*, John Offord, Eastbourne, 1979, p. 197.

12 Richard Hayhow's early community theatre work, for example, was based on such a view.

13 See the work of Augusto Boal, for example Augusto Boal, *Theatre of the Oppressed*, Theatre Communications Group, New York, 1985 [originally published in Argentina, 1973]. Alternatively, for an overview of his approaches and work, see Frances Babbage, *Augusto Boal*, Routledge, London and New York, 2004.

14 Johnston: *House of Games*, p. xii.

15 Ibid, p. xi.

16 Naseem Khan, 'The public-going theatre: community and ethnic theatre', in Sandy Craig (ed.), *Dreams and Deconstructions: Alternative Theatre in Britain*, Amber Lane Press, Ambergate, 1980, p. 64.

17 Heddon and Milling: *Devising Performance*, Chapter 5, ft 22, p. 245.

18 Nabil Shaban, quoted in Heddon and Milling: *Devising Performance*, p. 114.

19 See www.mind-the-gap.org.uk.

20 We refer to Jon Palmer's earlier work as Artistic Director of Interplay. Interplay continues to tour shows for audiences of people with learning disabilities under the direction of Steve Byrne, employing a self-contained dome which provides a cocoon for audiences, less than twenty at a time, to engage with a range of multi-sensory experiences incorporating puppetry and live music. They also take on residencies in schools and theatres.

21 Definition obtained from www.cmmc.nhs.uk/cancerinfo/glossaryl.asp, accessed 15 August 2008.

22 Individuals with Disabilities Education Act (IDEA), 2004.

23 Michael Oliver, *Understanding Disability: From Theory to Practice*, Palgrave Macmillan, Basingstoke and New York, 1996. p. 10.

II Authenticity

1 For both Brecht and Boal, empathising with the characters encourages unquestioning adherence to the 'truth' or ideology –Boal's 'finished visions of the world' – presented in the play.

2 Theories based on the psychoanalytic model and premised upon the existence of the unconscious are too numerous to list here. For histories of 'conscious' identity formation see, for example, the work of American psychologist Erving Goffman and that of contemporary writers on 'self-invention' such as Joanne Finkelstein. Various ideas on the formation of the self are also usefully discussed in relation to drama in Salvo

Pitruzzella's *Introduction to Dramatherapy: Person and Threshold*, Brunner-Routledge, Hove, 2004. Pitruzzella notes that contemporary 'group therapy' sessions are in effect an offshoot of the ideas of radical theatre practitioner Jacob Levi Moreno (1889–1974), a contemporary of Freud and founder of the 'Spontaneity Theatre'.

3   Breton's apparently autobiographical work *Nadja*, published in Paris in 1928, describes his meeting and liaison with a mysterious woman whose enigmatic and erratic behaviour and speech eventually lead to a breakdown and subsequent internment in an asylum.

4   Friedrich Nietzsche, *The Birth of Tragedy*, 1872.

5   Peter Brook, *The Empty Space*, Penguin Modern Classics, London, 2008, p. 60.

6   See André Green, *The Tragic Effect: The Oedipus Complex in Tragedy*, trans. Alan Sheridan, Cambridge University Press, Cambridge, 1979.

7   Antonin Artaud, *The Theatre and its Double*, trans. Victor Corti, Calder and Boyars, London, 1970, p. 42.

8   Ibid., p. 43.

9   Jerzy Grotowski, *Towards a Poor Theatre*, Routledge, New York, 2002, p. 255.

10 See Simon Shepherd and Mick Wallis, *Drama/Theatre/Performance*, Routledge, London, 2004, p. 59.

11 Grotowski: *Towards a Poor Theatre*, p. 16.

12 See Augusto Boal, *Theatre of the Oppressed*, Theatre Communications Group, New York, 1985.

13 Deirdre Heddon and Jane Milling, *Devising Performance: A Critical History*, Palgrave Macmillan, Basingstoke and New York, 2006, p. 63.

14 Antony Damasio has referred to this self-consciousness, this idea of 'knowing that we know', as 'extended' as opposed to 'core consciousness'. Self-consciousness, which is less pronounced in those with learning disabilities, can be a huge inhibitor of authentic behaviour and, by extension, authentic acting. For a detailed exposition of 'extended consciousness' see Antonio Damasio, *The Feeling of What Happens*, Vintage, London, 2000, pp. 195–233.

15 Heddon and Milling: *Devising Theatre*, p. 209.

16 Ibid.

17 Brook: *The Empty Space*, p. 62.

18 Anthony Howell and Fiona Templeton, *Elements of Performance Art*, Ting Books, London, 1977.

19 See Shepherd and Wallis: *Drama/Theatre/Performance* for an in-depth account of the history of the usage of the term.
20 Brook: *The Empty Space*, p. 57.
21 Ibid, p. 125.
22 Rachel Karafistan writing on The Shysters, 'Revisioning the Actor with Learning Disabilities', *New Theatre Quarterly*, March 2004, pp. 265–79.
23 *Musical Chairs*, Full Body and the Voice, performed on fourteen occasions between Autumn 2000 and Spring 2001.
24 These are terms by which learning disability is measured as defective in US legislation.
25 Vanessa Rosenthal, in interview on her work with Full Body and the Voice.

III Understanding the Person, Preparing the Actor

1 Dymphna Callery has outlined the notion of the 'creative actor' in her book *Through the Body: A Practical Guide to Physical Theatre*, Nick Hern Books, London, 2001.
2 Jacques Lecoq, *The Moving Body [Le Corps Poetique]*, trans. by David Bradby. Methuen, London, 2000, p. 9.
3 David Abram, *The Spell of the Sensuous*, Vintage, New York, 1997, p. 49.
4 Callery: *Through the Body*, p. 8.
5 See Arnold Mindell and Marie-Louise von Franz, *Dreambody: the Body's Role in Revealing the Self*, Lao Tse Press, Portland, OR, 1998.
6 Chris Johnston, *House of Games: Making Theatre from Everyday Life*, Nick Hern Books, London, 2005, p. 162.
7 Guy Dartnell, quoted in Johnston, 2005, p. 163.
8 At Full Body and the Voice this exercise was used as the starting point for every working day and could last anything up to an hour before moving into other areas of improvisation, devising or rehearsing.
9 Johnston: *House of Games*, p. 166.

IV Starting Points

1 Nabil Shaban, quoted in Deirdre Heddon and Jane Milling, *Devising Performance: A Critical History*, Palgrave Macmillan, Basingstoke and New York, 2006, pp. 115–116.
2 Quoted in Lizbeth Goodman, *Contemporary Feminist Theatres: To Each Her Own*, Routledge, London, 1993, p. 54.

3   This was certainly the case for Full Body and the Voice who in the first few years saw a number of people with 'moderate' learning disabilities come and go while the performers in the company with Down Syndrome remained in the majority and dictated the 'house style'.

4   Peter Brook, *The Empty Space*, Penguin Modern Classics, London, 2008, p. 11.

5   Jon Palmer's work with Interplay Theatre, Leeds.

6   IOU quoted in Alison Oddey, *Devising Theatre: A Practical and Theoretical Handbook*, Routledge, London and New York, 1994, p. 129.

7   The principal narrative of The Shysters' third show, *Tango Apocalypso*, 2003, was created entirely from working with a single CD.

8   *Sea Changes*, Interplay Theatre, 1995.

9   William Shakespeare, *The Tempest*, III. ii. 146.

10 Rose Myers, quoted in Deidre Heddon and Jane Milling, *Devising Performance: A Critical History*, Palgrave Macmillan, Basingstoke and New York, 2006, p. 146.

V Generating Material, Character and Narrative

1   Phelim McDermott in interview with the authors.

2   Julia Kristeva's understanding of poetics is as driven primarily by bodily rhythms (she refers to this as the semiotic, using the term in a rather different sense than that in which it is usually used) rather than the Symbolic realm of syntax, language and linear meaning. For Kristeva poetry in this way disrupts and exposes the Symbolic order. See Julia Kristeva, *Revolution in Poetic Language*, Columbia University Press, New York, 1984.

3   Both of these emotions – violence and random injustice – have fed into the work of The Shysters, as in *Scary Antics*, 1999 and *Fallen Angels*, 2000/2001.

VI Visual Theatre – Structure, Narrative, Meaning

1   Heddon and Milling note the difficulty with terminology here. Work that would in the 1980s have been termed 'visual theatre' now generally goes under the banner of 'performance'. See Deirdre Heddon and Jane Milling, *Devising Performance, A Critical History*, Palgrave Macmillan, Basingstoke and New York, 2006, p. 190.

2   Ibid., p. 78. Christine Entwistle was brought on board for *Play Dead*, 2004, though the People Show insist this did not mark a shift towards the use of an Artistic Director.

3 Emma Rice in interview with the authors.
4 Heddon and Milling: *Devising Performance*, p. 198.
5 See Anne Nesbet's *Savage Junctures: Sergei Eisenstein's and the Shape of Thinking*, I.B.Tauris, London, 2003.
6 Kristeva uses the term contrarily, as we have noted, ridding it of its usual structuralist reference to sign-systems.
7 See Sigrid Weigel's *Body- and Image-Space: Re-reading Walter Benjamin*, Routledge, London, 1996, for an extensive analysis of this frequently misunderstood area of Benjamin's thought.
8 Heddon and Milling: *Devising Performance*, p. 204.
9 Liz LeCompte, quoted in Nick Kaye, *Art into Theatre: Performance, Interviews and Documents*, Harwood Academic, Amsterdam, 1996, p. 257.
10 Chris Johnston, *House of Games*, Nick Hern Books, London, 2005, p. 198.
11 Heddon and Milling: *Devising Performance*, pp. 200–201.
12 Mark Long, quoted in Heddon and Milling: *Devising Performance*, p. 79.
13 *Off Limits*, Full Body and the Voice, 1999.
14 *Scene Changes*, Full Body and the Voice, 2004/2005.
15 Quoted in Heddon and Milling: *Devising Performance*, p. 78.

VII Performance, Professionalism and the Public

1 Research by University of California, Los Angeles.
2 In the early days of Full Body and the Voice Jon Palmer resisted showing work-in-progress as such. This was due to a concern about misconceptions around 'learning disability theatre' and amateurism. In retrospect there should be no reason why this approach, so common in drama schools, should not be taken.
3 In a production of *A Midsummer Night's Dream* in which some members of the Shysters played the Mechanicals, many audience members, commenting on how much they had enjoyed their performances, also asked the question, 'Who were those people?' It is a question we are unlikely to hear asked regarding actors generally.

Conclusion: Questions for the Future

1 Tom Shakespeare in interview with the authors.
2 Ibid.

Bibliography and Further Reading

Abram, David, *The Spell of the Sensuous*, Vintage Books, New York, 1997.
Artaud, Antonin, *The Theatre and its Double*, trans. Victor Corti, Calder and Boyars, London, 1970.
Babbage, Frances, *Augusto Boal*, Routledge, London and New York, 2004.
Barker, Clive, *Theatre Games: A New Approach to Drama Training*, Methuen, London, 1977.
Bates, Brian, *The Way of the Actor: A Path to Knowledge and Power*, Shambhala, Boston, MA, 1987.
Boal, Augusto, *Theatre of the Oppressed*, Theatre Communications Group, New York, 1985 [originally published in Argentina, 1973].
Brook, Peter, *The Empty Space*, Penguin Modern Classics, London, 1968, 1990, 2008.
Brook, Peter, *The Shifting Point: 40 years of Theatrical Exploration*, Methuen, London, 1987.
Brook, Peter, *There Are No Secrets: Thoughts on Acting and Theatre*, Methuen, London, 1993.
Callery, Dymphna, *Through the Body: A Practical Guide to Physical Theatre*, Nick Hern Books, London, 2001.
Campbell, Jane and Michael Oliver, *Disability Politics: Understanding our Past, Changing our Future*, Routledge, London and New York, 1996.

Coult, Tony and Baz Kershaw (eds), *Engineers of the Imagination: 'Welfare State' Handbook*, Methuen Drama, London and New York, 1983.

Damasio, Antonio, *The Feeling of What Happens*, Vintage, London, 2000.

Delgado, Maria M. and Paul Heritage (eds), *In Contact with the Gods? Directors Talk Theatre*, Manchester University Press, Manchester and New York, 1996.

Fortier, Mark, *Theory/Theatre: An Introduction*, Routledge, London and New York, 1997.

Giannachi, Gabriella and Mary Luckhurst (eds), *On Directing: Interviews with Directors*, Faber and Faber, London, 1999.

Goodman, Lizbeth, *Contemporary Feminist Theatres: To Each Her Own*, Routledge, London, 1993.

Green, André, *The Tragic Effect: The Oedipus Complex in Tragedy*, trans. Alan Sheridan, Cambridge University Press, Cambridge, 1979.

Grotowski, Jerzy, *Towards a Poor Theatre*, Routledge, New York, 2002.

Heddon, Deirdre and Jane Milling, *Devising Performance: A Critical History*, Palgrave MacMillan, Basingstoke and New York, 2006.

Heilpern, John, *Conference of the Birds*, Routledge, New York and London, 1999.

Howell, Anthony and Fiona Templeton, *Elements of Performance Art*, Ting Books, London, 1977.

Itzin, Catherine, *British Alternative Theatre Directory*, John Offord, Eastbourne, 1979.

Johnston, Chris, *House of Games: Making Theatre from Everyday Life*, Nick Hern Books, London, 1998, 2005.

Johnston, Chris, *The Improvisation Game: Discovering the Secrets of Spontaneous Performance*, Nick Hern Books, London, 2006.

Johnstone, Keith, *Impro: Improvisation and the Theatre*, Eyre Methuen, London, 1981.

Karafistan, Rachel, 'Revisioning the Actor with Learning Disabilities', *New Theatre Quarterly*, March 2004, pp. 265–79.

Kaye, Nick, *Art into Theatre: Performance, Interviews and Documents*, Harwood Academic, Amsterdam, 1996.

Kershaw, Baz, *The Radical in Performance: Between Brecht and Baudrillard*, Routledge, London and New York, 1999.

Khan, Naseem, 'The public-going theatre: community and ethnic theatre', in Sandy Craig (ed.), *Dreams and Deconstructions: Alternative Theatre in Britain*, Amber Lane Press, Ambergate, 1980.

Kristeva, Julia, *Revolution in Poetic Language*, Columbia University Press, New York, 1984.

Kuppers, Petra, *Petra, Disability and Contemporary Performance: Bodies on the Edge*, Routledge, New York and London, 2003.

Lecoq, Jacques, *The Moving Body [Le Corps Poetique]*, trans. by David Bradby. Methuen, London, 2000.

Mindell, Arnold and Marie-Louise von Franz, *Dreambody: The Body's Role in Revealing the Self*, Lao Tse Press, Portland, OR, 1998.

Nesbet, Anne, *Savage Junctures: Sergei Eisenstein's and the Shape of Thinking*, I.B.Tauris, London, 2003.

Oddey, Alison, *Devising Theatre: A Practical and Theoretical Handbook*, Routledge, London and New York, 1994, 2006.

Oida, Yoshi and Lorna Marshall, *The Invisible Actor*, Methuen, London, 1997.

Oliver, Michael *Understanding Disability: From Theory to Practice*, Palgrave Macmillan, Basingstoke and New York, 1996.

Pinker, Steven, *The Language Instinct*, Harper Perennial Modern Classics, London, 2007.

Pitruzzella, Salvo, *Introduction to Dramatherapy: Person and Threshold*, Brunner-Routledge, Hove, 2004.

Shakespeare, Tom, *Disability Rights and Wrongs*, Routledge, London and New York, 2006.

Shepherd, Simon and Mick Wallis, *Drama/Theatre/Performance*, Routledge, London and New York, 2004.

Weigel, Sigrid, *Body- and Image-Space: Re-reading Walter Benjamin*, Routledge, London, 1996.

Index

3D 27
7:84: 16, 23

A
Abram, David 73
Action Space Mobile 15
Age Exchange 16, 21
Agitprop Street Players 16
alcoholism 53
Amici Dance Theatre 96
applied theatre 176
Appollonian drive 36, 108
Arena Theatre 104
Aristotle 39
Artaud, Antonin 37, 40
Asperger's Syndrome 41, 94
autism 94

B
Babbage, Frances 26
Banner Theatre 20, 21
Barker, Clive 40
Beethoven, Ludwig van
    Fifth Symphony 96
Belgrade Theatre, Coventry 24

Belt and Braces 16, 20
Benjamin, Walter 137
Berman, Ed 15, 25
Birth of Tragedy, The 36
Blood Group 17, 18
Boal, Augusto 20, 22, 23, 27,
    33, 39, 44
Bradford Art College Theatre
    Group, The 16
Brecht, Bertolt 33, 38, 137, 138
Breton, Andre 35
Brook, Peter 18, 37, 46, 50, 64,
    90, 148, 178
Brooks, Louise 99
Brown, Susan 27
Bussell, Darcey 50
Butler, Judith 35
Byrne, Steve 28

C
Callery, Dymphna 59, 73
CAST 16, 20
Castiglione, Baldassare 34
Centre for International Theatre
    Research 18

Cheeseman, Peter 21
Children in Need 175
Cixous, Hélène 18
Cockin, Dorothy 178
Cockpit 24
commedia dell'arte 20, 101
Community Arts 176
Community Play, the 21
community theatre 13, 21, 40, 153
Complicite 19
Conference of the Birds 18
Constructivists, the 136
copying 76–9, 81

D

Damasio, Antony 43
Dartnell, Guy 79, 82
Death in Venice 96
Descartes, René 44
de-socialisation 36
Down Syndrome 51, 53, 93, 144, 166, 174, 175
drama therapy 22, 27, 73, 153
Dyonisian drive 36, 108

E

Eccleston, Christopher 178
Eisenstein, Sergei 135
Emin, Tracey 161
empathy 67, 75–8, 80
Entwistle, Christine 127
Ernst, Max 138
European funding 180

F

feminism 50
Figgis, Mike 160
Figment Theatre 104
film 34, 53, 91, 99, 125, 132, 135, 160
Finkelstein, Joanne 35
First Movement 28
Flesh and Blood 178
Forced Entertainment 44
Forkbeard Fantasy 102
Forum Theatre 22, 27
Franz, Marie-Louise von 73, 76
Freud, Sigmund 35, 108
Full Body and the Voice 163, 181
    Musical Chairs 47,
    Off Limits 141
    Scene Changes 142
Furse, Anna 18

G

Gainsborough, Thomas 136
Gay Sweatshop 16
Glass, Philip
    Violin Concerto 97
Goat Island 138
Goddard, Janet 103
Goffman, Erving 35
Goodman, Lizbeth 100
Graeae 12, 27, 86
Grandin, Temple 42
Green, André 37
Greenwich Young People's Theatre 24
Grotowski, Jerzy 38–9
Grove, Claire 86

H

Happenings 17, 45
Heart and Soul 180
Heartfield, John 138
Heddon, Deirdre 16, 19, 26, 40, 44, 104, 127, 134, 139, 140
Hesitate and Demonstrate 17, 103
Hopper, Edward 103
Howell, Anthony 53

I

Icy Tea 21
Impressionists, the 136
Improbable Theatre 116
Inter Action 15, 20, 21, 25
Interplay 15, 28, 92
  Sea Changes 103
Irigaray, Luce 18
IOU 17, 95
  A Drop in the Ocean 102

J

Jackson, Glenda 116
Jellico, Ann 21
Johnston, Chris 20, 23, 40, 76, 80, 93, 139
Johnstone, Keith 15, 20
Judd, Donald 136
Jung, Carl Gustav 117

K

Kabuki Theatre 162
Karafistan, Rachel 47
Khan, Naseem 25, 42

Kirby, Peter 178
Kneehigh Theatre 127
Kristeva, Julia 18, 119, 137

L

Laban technique 59
Lacan, Jacques 73
Lawnmowers, The 28
Learning Disabilities Association of America, The 28, 51
Le Compte, Liz 138, 139
Le Coq, Jacques 19, 72, 101
Leeds TIE 24
libido 36
Ling, Geraldine 27
Living Theatre 45
Loach, Ken 48
Long, Mark 141, 143
Lumiere and Son 102

M

Macchiaioli, the 136
MacMillan, Kenneth 50
Major Road 102
Mahler, Gustav 96
Man with a Movie Camera 135
McDermott, Phelim 82, 116
mental illness 53
Merleau-Ponty, Maurice 44, 73
method acting 34, 37–8, 46
Meyerhold, Vsevolod 38
Milling, Jane 16, 19, 26, 40, 44, 104, 127, 134, 139, 140
Mind the Gap 27
Mindell, Arnold 73, 76

minimalism 136
mirroring 69, 75
Monstrous Regiment 16
Moreno, Jacob Levi 35
multi-sensory rooms 92
music 87, 95–101, 139
Mutable Theatre 16
Myers, Rose 104

N
Nadja 36
New Vic, Stoke-on-Trent 21, 177
national curriculum, the 24
National Health Service 29
Nesbet, Anne 136
Nietzsche, Friedrich 36, 37, 108
Nicholson, Helen 24
Night Hawks 103
non-verbal communication 62, 74
normativity 42
North West Spanner 16

O
Oily Cart 28
Oliver, Michael 28
Out of Joint 177

P
Pandora's Box 99
People Show, the 16, 45, 103, 126, 127, 141, 143, 160
percussion instruments 100
performance art 40, 45, 116

phenomenology 73
Pilgrim, Geraldine 103
Pinocchio 91, 141
Pinker, Steven 18
Pitruzzella, Salvo 35
Pointillists, the 136
Pollock, Jackson 133
profound and multiple learning disabilities 94
props 65, 80–1, 87, 91, 92, 143
psychoanalysis 73
psychodrama 73

R
rapport 67, 69, 75, 89
Recreation Ground 20
Red Ladder 16
Reminiscence Theatre 21
Rice, Emma 127, 131
role-play 22
Rosenthal, Vanessa 55
Rousseau, Jean-Jaques 34

S
scriptwriter 38
semiotic, the 137
sensory rooms 14
SFX Theatre Company 27
Shaban, Nabil 27, 86
Shakespeare, Tom 175
Shakespeare, William 33, 147
    A Midsummer Night's Dream 97
    The Tempest 103
Shepherd, Simon 39, 45

Shysters, The 114, 181
   A Midsummer Night's Dream 166
   Fallen Angels 119
   Scary Antics 119
Sideshow 27
silent cinema 99
Siren 16
social model 12
socialisation 40
Song of the Earth 50
Sphinx 16
Stange, Wolfgang 96
Stanislavski, Constantin 37, 44, 116
Street Arts Community Theatre Company 21
Surrealism 35, 38
Surrealists, the 35, 37
Susumu's Story 24
Sutherland, Donald 159
symbolic, the 137

T

Templeton, Fiona 53
Theatre Centre 24, 177
theatre-in-education (TIE) 13, 24
Theatre of the Oppressed 20, 39
Theatre of Mistakes, the 17, 45, 136
The Empty Space 53, 55, 105
Titian 136
Tomlinson, Richard 27

U

Unity Theatre 16

V

Vertov, Djiga 135
Visconti, Luchino 96

W

Wallis, Mick 39, 45
Weigel, Sigrid 137
Welfare State International 16, 102
Wheeler, Tim 27
Wilson, Robert 17
Women's Theatre Group 16, 86
Wooster Group, The 138, 139
Word and Action (Dorset) 20, 21